THE ACTUALITY
OF ATONEMENT

THE ACTUALITY
OF ATONEMENT

A Study of Metaphor, Rationality and the
Christian Tradition

Colin E. Gunton

T&T CLARK
EDINBURGH

T&T CLARK LTD
59 GEORGE STREET
EDINBURGH EH2 2LQ
SCOTLAND

www.tandtclark.co.uk

First published 1988
Latest impression 2000

ISBN 0 567 29220 7

British Library Cataloguing-in-Publication Data
A catalogue record for this book is available from the British Library

Printed and bound in Great Britain by Redwood Books, Wiltshire

In Memoriam

George Bradford Caird
1917-1984

Vivian Gerald Hines
1912-1987

CONTENTS

PREFACE

In his *The Atonement and the Sacraments* (1961, p.216), Robert S. Paul remarked that 'When Horace Bushnell spoke of an annual harvest of books on the Atonement, he was perhaps exaggerating, but by the end of the nineteenth century this was becoming literal fact.' It was not very different with the years between then and the publication of Professor Paul's book, which closely followed J.S. Whale's splendid *Victor and Victim*, one of the inspirations for this study. Since then, however, the flood has declined to a trickle. Perhaps the one major theological study in English has been F.W. Dillistone's *The Christian Understanding of Atonement*, recently reprinted, but now nearly twenty years old. Indeed, it has recently been argued, in the article by Colin Grant so entitled, that there has taken place 'The Abandonment of Atonement' (Grant 1986). Other matters have taken priority, among them a preoccupation with Christianity's moral and social responsibilities.

Important as the latter are, however, the church will be reduced to empty rhetoric and mindless conformist activism unless it is rooted in a living tradition of worship and praise, centred on the cross and resurrection of Jesus. Christianity is good news, gospel, not because it offers final solutions to the problems of the inner city (or whatever), though there is no doubt that it has much to say to those who live both at the centre and at the margins of our society, but because it proclaims and lives from a prior and redeeming act of God in Jesus Christ.

It is not being denied, however, that as the product of a particular time and place this book, like all theology, takes shape in a particular context, so that an attempt to reopen an apparently closed question should not be seen as a bolt from the blue. Alongside our contemporary preoccupation with social ethics is another, that of the very possibility and nature of speech about God. In this area, there have been studies of metaphor, and of the way it can be conceived to create possibilities for theology. But none, so far, have examined the metaphors in which our understanding of salvation, and therefore of who God is and we are, has been couched.

Although theologians are among the last to realise it, there has been in recent years something of a sea-change in the way in which the Enlightenment's heritage has been received in our culture, and the opening chapters of this book take up in a different place the theme of Enlightenment and Alienation. In them there are charted some of the reasons why the verdict of an earlier generation on the Christian theology of salvation should not be taken as final, or even credible. These chapters locate the book in contemporary debate, but use such contextualisation as a springboard first for going far beyond the terms of that debate, and then for returning to the real context of theology, the worship, life and mission of the church.

By using the system of references that I have, I have tried to avoid the tedium of excessive footnoting and at the same time to give credit where possible to those to whom I owe much of the content of the work. Theology being what it is, an essentially communal and conversational discipline, there will be much that I have received from books and words that is not given due acknowledgement. For that I would apologise, but, more especially, thank all who have contributed to the process. Among those especially are

Daniel Hardy, who has contributed in different ways to all stages, and to Christoph Schwöbel, who read a nearly final draft and made valuable comments and suggestions.

Thanks are due also to Geoffrey Green and his colleagues at T & T Clark for much encouragement and assistance, and to Sarah and Carolyn Gunton for meticulous and perceptive reading of proofs.

The book is gratefully dedicated to the memory of two who have died during its writing. The influence of George Caird, interpreter of the Bible, will be manifest in many places; that of my uncle, Vivian Hines, less obvious but equally important.

Colin Gunton
Brentwood, Essex
October 1988

ACKNOWLEDGEMENTS

The author wishes to acknowledge permission to re-use in parts of Chapters 2, 3, 4 and 5 material which first appeared in the following works:

'Christus Victor Revisited. A Study in Metaphor and the Transformation of Meaning.' *Journal of Theological Studies* 36, 1985, Oxford University Press, pp.129-145

'Christ the Sacrifice. Aspects of the Language and Imagery of the Bible.' *The Glory of Christ in the New Testament.* Edited by L.D. Hurst and N.T. Wright, Oxford University Press, pp. 229-238

'The Justice of God.' *Free Church Chronicle* 40, 1985, Free Church Federal Council, pp. 13-19

1

Patterns of Rationalism

There are more things in heaven and earth,
Horatio,
Than are dreamt of in your philosophy.
Shakespeare, Hamlet, I.V.166

I Where We Stand

As he wrestled with the legacy of the Age of Reason, Samuel Taylor Coleridge became convinced that some of his predecessors had, in the name of reason, effectively reduced that supreme human capacity to a mere shadow of its real self. Once conceived as the endowment whereby we are able to engage with the mysteries of our life in the universe, human reason had been reduced to little more than the means of calculating the relation of means and ends. More than a century and a half later, partly because other guides than Coleridge have been followed, we still live with the consequences of the virtual reduction of reason to a narrowly conceived process of reasoning. The result is that our vision is narrowed and our culture impoverished, so that if a belief or practice cannot be shown to be reasonable according to certain highly restricted canons of judgement, it will be dismissed without due consideration of its claims.

How shall we avoid the intellectual and cultural poverty that remains so much a feature of our age, perhaps especially of what remains of its theology? The first lesson to learn is that rationalism is one thing, the claims of a reason that wishes to encompass life in its richness quite another. Rationalism's desire is to restrict all human response to the world within a Procrustean bed, defining in advance what may or may not be said. A quest for the due rationality of things, on the other hand, will pay due respect to the implications of Hamlet's famous dictum. It will seek to encompass the sheer range, flexibility and variety of human interaction with the world. In such an enterprise, to be rational will be to allow the manifold features of our experience to be given due place in our thinking about who and what we are, and about what is the nature of the universe in which we are set.

The Christian doctrine of the atonement, an area of theological thought which has been much neglected in recent years, provides an ideal subject for a study of the nature of human rationality. *Atonement* is the portmanteau word used in English to denote the reconciliation between God and the world which is the heart of Christian teaching. It is an ideal subject because it encompasses so many features of human experience, the rational narrowly conceived as well as the ethical and aesthetic. Another advantage is that it is a part of theology which is inseparably connected with life in the church and in the world, and therefore cannot be adequately treated without reference to action as well as theory. (Not that any area of Christian theology can be adequately treated in a merely theoretical way.) Yet more encouragement is provided by the fact that traditional expressions of the teaching have been those to suffer most seriously at the hands of rationalist critics. Many aspects of the theology of the atonement, as they were formulated in the centuries before the modern era, have been argued to violate modern canons of morality, rationality, and truth. The criticisms, like the formulations of the doctrine, take us into many aspects of human thought and life, involving as they do beliefs about language, knowledge, history and ethics. Some of them are justified, but many derive from a tendency to overstress the power of the human intellect. Accordingly, the first main stage of this enquiry will be to ask how traditional conceptions of the atonement have been affected by rationalist criticism. In it we shall follow the thought of three great modern thinkers to show how they treat different aspects of the inherited teaching.

II Redemption by Reason: Immanuel Kant and the Rationalism of Morality

One dimension of human experience centrally at stake in the discussion of the atonement is the ethical. Christian teaching has been founded on a doctrine of the helplessness, apart from God's new initiative – apart from redemption, that is to say – of the human agent. Doctrines of the fall have been used to demonstrate this helplessness, and although they have sometimes, particularly in the West, depended on a belief in the historical existence of a first human pair, that is not their chief point. That, rather, has been to show that the human plight is so serious that only the personal presence of God in Christ and an atoning death on the cross can bring it healing and completeness. The extent of this ethical helplessness has often been a matter of debate, especially in the famous dispute between Augustine and Pelagius, but also at the Reformation. The Augustinian and Reformation traditions alike teach a radical fallenness, and the corresponding need for a historical redemption. It is to this teaching that modern rationalism, which tends to be tied to an optimistic belief in human capabilities, has taken severest exception. Its response has taken two related forms, the intellectual and the practical. From an intellectual point of view it has been claimed that, far from being fallen, the human mind has innate within it the capacity to discover without assistance from any authority outside itself a code of behaviour adequate to the needs of life in the world. In this respect, the seeds of later rationalism are to be found in the mediaeval

3

natural law theory that unaided reason was able to discover universal moral truths. With the Enlightenment, the seeds grew into the full plant, so that John Locke believed that all moral laws were discoverable by unaided reason:

> I am bold to think that morality is capable of demonstration... since the precise real essence of the things moral words stand for may be perfectly known, and so the congruity and incongruity of the things themselves be perfectly discovered: in which consists perfect knowledge. (*Essay* III. xi. 16)

Similar claims came to be made for the practical realm. The confidence in human capacity was sometimes extended so far as to claim that inherent in what may be called the rational will is the capacity not only to discover but also to carry out the requirements of morality. The Enlightenment in that way produced a radical version of the Pelagianism against which Augustine had struggled. Whether or not Pelagius was guilty of the heresy which bears his name, there is little doubt that his modern successors have come to believe that we may realise our humanity without divine grace, healing or redemption. That belief, in its turn, is the cause of the sense of unreality – and hence irrationality – that attends so many modern discussions of ethical matters.

In all this, the central concept for our purposes is *autonomy*, the doctrine that each person is individually and completely responsible for moral action and should be free of all 'external' authorities like tradition and the church. Immanuel Kant (1724-1804) is a crucial figure in the development of the modern doctrine, largely because he was a rationalist who was aware of the weaknesses of rationalism. In the works devoted primarily to ethics, Kant's thought is rationalistic in both of the senses outlined above. Responsibility for the discovery and carrying into practice of the maxims of behaviour belongs to the individual agent alone. However, in *Religion Within the Limits of Reason Alone* (Kant 1794/1960), Kant gives an account of the moral agent which is carefully qualified to avoid the pitfalls of a naïvely optimistic theory. In fact, he is scornful of moral optimism. 'That such a corrupt propensity must indeed be rooted in man need not be formally proved in view of the multitude of crying examples which experience *of the actions* of men puts before our eyes' (p.28). The facts speak for themselves: there is too much evidence to the contrary for any naïve optimism about human capacity.

It is not the place here to go in detail into Kant's doctrine of radical evil, save to say that it is a carefully formulated philosophical translation of the traditional Western Christian doctrine of original sin. According to it, the origin of moral evil is a rationally inexplicable ('inscrutable', p.38) perversion of our will, whereby we come to prefer evil maxims of behaviour to good ones. Along with orthodox Christianity Kant avoids the Manichaean doctrine that we or the material world are evil in ourselves, though it has to be said that, also in common with the tradition, he comes close to it on occasions. The root of human moral evil lies rather in the corruption of what is essentially good. His reason, again, is much the same as that of orthodox Christianity, for he believes in the redeemability of that which has become evil. Where Kant differs decisively from the tradition to which he is so closely related is in his view of what that redemption is and how it takes place. Moving through one hundred and eighty degrees in relation to the Lutheranism in his past, he ascribes it not to God through faith in the justifying death of Christ but to God operating through human moral reason. As the title of his book implies, its programme is an account of religion as rational and that alone.

How, then, is redemption achieved? It is, in Kant's own words, 'through one's own exertions' (p.46). He is insistent that we are able to do what the moral law instructs, and is able so to insist because he is a rationalist in the narrower sense of the word. He holds that what is discoverable by reason operating by its own resources alone must be the truth. 'For when the moral law' – and by that he means the law which human practical reason has discovered for itself – 'commands that we *ought* now to be better men, it follows that we must *be able* to be better men' (p.46, cf p.56). Here is Kant's wide difference from the orthodox doctrine of the fall, which holds precisely that we *are not able* to be better, even though we know that we ought. The outcome of this lack of realism is that the salvation ascribed by historic Christianity to the action of God in the person of Jesus Christ is transferred by Kant to the action of the rational moral agent: hence the reference to the one hundred and eighty degree change of direction. There could be no more complete about face. The irony, although it is also an important indication of what he is doing, is that in the process Kant draws upon biblical and theological language in order to describe the content of the salvation that is to be achieved. Of particular interest for our purposes is the fact that he uses terms which will be recognised by those who are familiar with formulations of the traditional doctrine of the atonement. There is, for example, the language of sacrifice: 'The coming forth from the corrupted into the good disposition is, in itself (as "the death of the old man", "the crucifying of the flesh"), a sacrifice...' (p.68). Traditional terms like *satisfaction* and *justification* (p.70) are also used, but to describe not the act of God in the cross of Jesus but the human moral struggle and rebirth *symbolised by* the cross. The teaching is not that of a religion of redemption, but of a moral philosophy – one of redemption, indeed, but of redemption achieved through the re-activation of the innate powers of the moral will.

The overall effect of Kant's work, accordingly, is a transmogrification of Christianity into its opposite. There are, without doubt, tensions within the work which make it unjust to say that without qualification, for, as the biblical quotations show and as Barth has asked, 'Is it possible with impunity to be so far in agreement with St. Paul as Kant after all was in his doctrine of sin?' (Barth 1952/1972 p.297) Moreover, Kant did see redemption taking place by means of a divine activity: the difference, and it is all the difference in the world, was that God is to be found in human moral reason and action, not encountered as a personal creator and redeemer. The general drift is clear: to a moral rationalism which either throws into question or fundamentally alters the meaning of the language Christians had used until the modern era. If we are saved from radical moral evil by our innate capacity, we do not need to be saved by the cross because we save ourselves, albeit with the assistance of a God located within ourselves.

This outline of aspects of Kant's moral philosophy has not been presented merely as a lament over the way in which Christianity has by it been reduced to something else. Rather, Kant presents us with two questions which must be answered if we are to continue to hold to a version of the traditional teaching. The first concerns the nature of the human moral agent. Can we be saved by another agency, God's or anyone else's, without the loss of our moral freedom and autonomy? Is Christianity bound to be a religion of 'heteronomy', saving us only at the expense of depriving us of our freedom or making us moral infants? That is the charge frequently levelled by modern rational-ism, and it is not one that can be ignored, if only because the Christian faith has always understood itself as a means to

7

human liberation. What else should be the heart of redemption, a metaphor deriving from the freeing of slaves? Where then is real freedom? In Christ, who meets us as another, as God made man? (See, for example, John 8.36: 'if the Son makes you free, you will be free indeed'.) Or is freedom, in despite of all the evidence, already inherent within us?

Second, Kant faces us with the question of our relation to the past. If there is to be human salvation, it must concern us as we live in the present, and that means that some account must be given of how we are related to the past events which we consider so crucial. One of the tasks that Kant was attempting in his work was a reinterpretation of the biblical text in order to free it from the trammels of the past. Hans Frei has shown something of the extent of Kant's achievement. 'For Kant the meaning of the biblical narratives was strictly a matter of understanding the ideas they represent in story form... (H)e does his best to reinterpret... the concepts and stories derived from biblical and traditional Christian usage' (Frei 1974 pp.262f). From one point of view, Kant has done no more than many others have done and are doing, and what must be done if the theological task is to be taken seriously. It is not the enterprise but the way in which he appears to have carried it out that is the problem. If Kant's rationalism in effect translates Christianity into its opposite, can that be a rational or reasonable way to read the foundational texts? But that, in its turn, raises another question. Do we have in the modern world the resources for a more adequate interpretation? Before we begin an answer to that question, we must take note of the fact that Kant does not stand alone in his attempted translation of the Christian tradition into the conditions of modernity. He was succeeded by two equally great theological minds, the first of whom, F.D.E. Schleiermacher (1768-1834), provides our next subject.

III   Translation and Reduction: F.D.E. Schleiermacher and the Rationalism of Experience

Part of Schleiermacher's greatness consists in the fact that he was alive to the challenges offered to theology by the thought of Kant. He therefore argued that Christianity was a religion of redemption which could not be reduced to reason, morality or a combination of the two. Salvation derived from the historical Jesus of Nazareth and, far from being the achievement of autonomous individuals, took shape only in a historical community. Moreover, Schleiermacher differed from Kant in wishing to avoid any suggestion of self-salvation, for he believed that Pelagianism was one of the basic Christian heresies. In other ways, however, he must be judged to have produced a rationalism which in its outcome, if not always in his own work, served only to transfer the problems of Kant's Enlightenment rationalism on to another plane.

The reason for the two-sidedness of that assessment of Schleiermacher lies in the fact that his was a two-sided response to Kant. On the one hand, he went beyond Kant, seeking to ground Christian theology in an aspect of the human relation to the world which had been given a relatively minor role by Kant. In that respect he provided for theology a far broader base than had been allowed it by the critical philosophy. On the other hand, Schleiermacher's theology operated within a rational framework largely provided by Kant, a framework which he buckled but never quite succeeded in breaking open. The development was roughly as follows. For Kant there were two areas in which human mental powers could claim a measure of success, although even there under strict limits. There could be knowledge of the world – broadly, factual knowledge – but only of that aspect of it which presented itself to sense experience, what he called the phenomena. The mind could

9

not penetrate beyond these appearances, but understand them only as it ordered them in accordance with concepts which, Kant held, belonged not to the world itself, but only to the mind's way of ordering its experience of the world. The world in itself could not be known, nor, *a fortiori*, could there be any knowledge of a God supposed to be the creator of that world. The second area where reason operated was, as we have seen, the practical, and here there was greater success, because the mind legislated autonomously for what ought to be. The maxims for right action could be discovered with certainty, and in the process even suggested reasons for belief in the existence of God, but, again, gave no knowledge of what God was in himself.

The heart of Schleiermacher's relation to Kant is to be found in the different interpretations the two gave to the third area of human experience, the aesthetic. For Kant, knowledge was not to be found in our experience of beauty. Aesthetic judgements did perform a valuable function in providing some link between the two other areas of experience, the factual and the ethical, but only subjectively (Kant 1793/1951 p.65). The reason is that we make aesthetic judgements by feeling, yet feeling 'teaches us absolutely nothing, but is merely the way in which the subject is affected as regards pleasure or displeasure' (Kant 1794/1960 p.105). We have a faculty called feeling, and we wish by its means to link the otherwise completely disparate realms of science and ethics, but are forbidden to regard it as the source of insight into the way the world actually is.

Schleiermacher did not question Kant's limitation of the capacity of pure reason to the phenomenal world and he shared his high valuation of ethical reasoning. In that respect, he operated within a strongly Kantian framework. Where he went beyond Kant was in developing the third, aesthetic, dimension of human experience. He did it by first denying Kant's doctrine that feeling teaches us nothing and then by strengthening and extending its function. Kant had never solved the problem of the relation between the factual and the ethical: they were left as two faculties whose relation could not be accounted for, and bequeathed to the modern world in the form of a kind of intellectual schizophrenia. Schleiermacher believed that the dualism could be avoided by elevating feeling above both pure and practical reason, which it unified in a higher synthesis. We can feel together what we cannot satisfactorily think together.

The outcome is a theology which is not rationalistic in the manner of Kant and his predecessors. Because feeling is prior to thought, the stress is on that which is above reason. Religion belongs in the realm of the suprarational, and theology is subordinate to it as the rational exposition of what is essentially above reason (see especially Schleiermacher 1830/1928 §13, Postscript). The rather paradoxical outcome, however, is a highly rationalistic account of the content of theological writing. Because the foundational experience is beyond or above reason, it is the more necessary to give its exposition a strongly formal literary structure. The very lack of a rational object – the object being one which is essentially *above* reason – makes it all the more necessary that what is written be under tight conceptual control. That is one reason why with Schleiermacher we reach the era of the system, in which the different topics of theology are ordered in a very tight logical relation to each other: 'manifestly, this can only reach a satisfactory conclusion when the system of doctrine has become a complete system, in which... all the dogmatic propositions are brought into relation with each other' (p.87).

Nor is it an accident that Schleiermacher accepts many of the rationalist criticisms of the form of traditional Christian teaching, for example, the classical christological formulations. The shift that he makes in his understanding of theology from the exposition of doctrine to the articulation of the content of experience in many respects concedes the case to the rationalist critique, particularly in its acceptance of the Kantian teaching that we can know nothing of the world and God as they are in themselves. Such a shift makes it inevitable that the content of Christian teaching will be, if not reduced to something else, at least expressed in a different form. The question then will be the same as it was in the case of Kant: Is the shift involved in the translation so great that in effect a new theology is created? And, again, the answer must be that although in Schleiermacher some of the language of Western atonement theology appears fairly prominently, it ceases to mean what it once did.

The character of the change is revealed by what happens to the legal metaphors that had been so much a feature of Christian theology, from Paul onwards. As we shall see, this approach to the theology of the atonement had achieved formal expression in the work of Anselm of Canterbury and in the Reformation tradition which owed much to him. In the centuries before Schleiermacher, however, Socinian and other rationalist critics of the tradition had taken strong exception to the penal language of Western atonement theology. That the death of Jesus should be understood as the suffering of a penalty owed to God in exchange for human sin seemed to them for many reasons, some of them good ones, both morally and rationally abhorrent. Schleiermacher shares their view that neither sin nor the cross should be understood in penal terms.

One reason for Schleiermacher's rejection of an important aspect of the Western tradition is to be found in his conception of the relation of God to the world. He is a platonist in the sense that he understands the action of God in and towards the world to be rather like that of an eternal form, timelessly embodying certain possibilities for the world of time. That is not to say that he has no room for a conception of the particular historical action of God in Jesus, but that the particularities tend to be overmastered by the general scheme within which they are set. In the theology of redemption, it works out somewhat as follows. God's action operates towards the human world in terms of what Schleiermacher calls 'person-forming', and redemption from sin is mainly to be seen as 'a continuation of that person-forming divine influence' (p.427). The advantage of speaking in this way is that continuity is maintained between the action of God in creation and redemption, and Schleiermacher's theology is sometimes in this respect likened to that of Irenaeus. Where he differs from the tradition (including Irenaeus), however, is in failing to hold to its teaching that on the cross Jesus in some way or other underwent the divine judgement on human sin. The cross is not in that way central to Schleiermacher's christology, which stresses much more strongly the work of the historical Jesus in transmitting to an organic religious community the consciousness of God which he himself possessed in a unique and exemplary manner.

Accordingly, the differences between Schleiermacher and the doctrine that had for the most part prevailed until his time are twofold. First, he believed that the resurrection, ascension and return of Christ in judgement are not 'properly constituent parts of the doctrine of His Person' (§99). The resurrection and ascension of Jesus had served as a way of showing how the past historical Jesus was also a living reality, present to church and world. Schleiermacher, having for various reasons abandoned that way of speaking, now throws the weight of his interpretation on the influence, mediated through the community, of the past Jesus of

13

Nazareth. Second, and of more direct interest for this chapter, his was a mainly exemplarist interpretation of Jesus' sufferings: that is to say, they are of importance more as an example to follow than as altering objectively our standing before God. It is not, he says 'proper to ascribe... a special reconciling value to His physical sufferings'; rather, '(t)he climax of His suffering... was sympathy with misery' (pp.437,436).

The outcome of all this is that the penal language does not disappear, but is interpreted experientially. It is taken to mean not that God is to be conceived as judge of human sin, but that outside the person-forming influence of the redeemer we experience sin as punishment. In this Schleiermacher is like Kant in wanting to reinterpret and not destroy the tradition, and so claims that the *real meaning* ('by the substitution of equivalents') of the teaching that 'through the suffering of Christ punishment is abolished' is that 'the evil which is in process of disappearing is no longer... regarded as punishment' (p.458). The gospel, that is to say, frees us from regarding the evil we experience as some kind of penalty for sin. Schleiermacher makes similar translations of other of the traditional concepts of atonement, that of 'satisfaction', for example, being understood in terms of Christ's being 'the eternally inexhaustible source, adequate for every further development, of a spiritual and blessed life.' Such 'satisfaction', he says, demolishing another pillar of the tradition, is 'in no sense "vicarious"' (p.461). Jesus does not die on our behalf, as our representative or in our place, or at least not in any sense that would be recognised as adequate by previous Western theologians, Catholic and Reformed alike.

Schleiermacher's great achievement in this sphere, and particularly in the perceptive account he develops of the corporate nature of both sin and salvation, should not be denied. Moreover, there is no doubt that there is much wrong with the Western tradition's preoccupation with the penal aspects of the atonement. Yet there can also be little doubt that this theologian has produced a reductionist account of the doctrine, reductionist in the sense that he changes the meaning of key concepts into something else. That is a mark of rationalism, one of whose symptoms is a refusal to accept concepts, particularly those adjudged 'anthropomorphic', for what they say and an attempt to change them into something else. That is not to claim that some original meaning can be found and kept totally sacrosanct, immune from change. Language is not like that. But it is also true that there comes a time when the meaning is changed so much that a word is made to say something entirely different, so that the tradition is not interpreted but broken. One of the ways in which this can be laid at Schleiermacher's door is by noting that he has produced a strongly subjectivist interpretation of traditional doctrines, so that their meaning is realised more in the experience of the Christian than with reference to the historical incarnation and cross. As in the case of Kant, they are more to do with something that happens within us than with the redeeming initiative of a free and transcendent God.

Given that the change has been made, however, we must ask as we did with Kant, what questions the development asks of those who would take leave to question its adequacy. The chief one would appear to be this: Does the language of law, punishment and penalty provide a suitable vocabulary in which to speak of the relationship between God and his people? To abandon it would be to lose not only a central theme of biblical witness – beginning with Paul's great treatise in Romans – but also much of what the Christian tradition has made of it. Yet it is right to subject the language to rational examination if we are not to succumb to a corresponding rationalism of 'orthodoxy'. The question of how best we should be loyal to the tradition is a real one, and Schleiermacher faces us with it. To anticipate later discussion, it can be said that here we are presented with the question of the metaphorical use of language. When theologians use the language of law, judgement and penalty they are using concepts taken from human legal institutions and using them to speak of the relation between God and the world. How realistically or literally are they to be construed? Schleiermacher's answer, and that of those who have followed him, is 'Scarcely at all.' There is no objective law or justice, and we must therefore speak only or chiefly of an inner human transformation. The reply of their conservative opponents has been to develop an equally rationalistic theory of what has come to be called penal substitution. I shall hope to show that neither side is right, and that if we misunderstand the metaphorical nature of the language, either explaining it away or taking it with narrow literalism, we shall not understand the content of the teaching. There is a case for the realistic use of the language of law and penalty, but it must be used in such a way that it takes account both of the objections that Schleiermacher and others have made and – more important – of the particular relationships the terms are intended to convey.

IV Metaphor and Concept: Hegel and Conceptual Rationalism

In the second section of this chapter we met, in the person of Kant, a rationalism of the moral agent; in the third, with Schleiermacher, a form of rationalism of experience, the effect of which is to emasculate traditional doctrines of the atonement, destroying their base in the historic redemptive action of God and producing a reductionist account of their language. Now we come to what is best called conceptual rationalism, which is a third way of limiting and narrowing the way in which words may be conceived to express meaning and truth. It has long been held that some ways of expressing meaning and truth are superior to others, often that particular kinds of word are the only ones truly fitted to show things as they are. One favourite way of showing this is to argue that meaning and truth are successfully conveyed only by means of concepts of an intellectual kind which have been purified as completely as possible from all imaginative or pictorial content. On such an account, concepts are strictly distinguished from and opposed to pictures and images: while the former are fitted to convey truth, the latter are, because of their unclarity, the source of deceit and confusion. Both Plato and Augustine were strongly attracted to versions of this doctrine, largely because they believed that information conveyed by the senses was inherently untrustworthy. The father of the modern variation on the theme is Descartes, who held that anything he could conceive with utter clarity and distinctness was true, anything less than that essentially unreliable.

The outcome of the teaching has been both an overvaluing of abstract logical connections between ideas and an undervaluing of everything else. In particular, it has been held that concepts with fuzzy edges or pictorial and imaginative content are not the best ways of expressing truth. The next chapter of this book is designed to demonstrate the opposite: that metaphor above all is an indispensable means for the advance of knowledge and understanding. Such a demonstration is necessary because, in its absence, the 'official' doctrine gives the doctrine of the atonement a hard time. All the main ways of spelling out the saving significance of the life, death and resurrection of Jesus contain a considerable metaphorical and imaginative content, drawing, as is often remarked, from a number of human institutions: notably the legal system, the altar of sacrifice, the battlefield and the slavemarket (see Whale 1960). Although it is possible to give the doctrines deriving from the metaphors systematic expression, they are intellectually suspect so long as they remain dependent on the images that are their source. The result is that the doctrine of the atonement, dependent as it is upon a particular historical story and the way it has been transmitted, has been a favourite candidate for rational criticism. The main images have been argued or refined away, leaving conceptions of the atonement which place the emphasis not on the significance of what happened with Jesus, but on the response of the believer. Response is without doubt an essential part of the overall picture, but without its being based in the prior grace of God, the Pelagianism that we have already met is the inevitable outcome. It was a tendency which was at work in Schleiermacher, although in his case it was to some extent mitigated by the emphasis he gave to the prior historical movement of God taking form in the life of the organic Christian community.

The conceptual rationalism of G.W.F. Hegel (1770-1831), subtle and carefully qualified as it is, provides an excellent opportunity to examine the kind of damage that can be inflicted on the content of Christian theology. James Yerkes has observed that central to an understanding of Hegel's christology is a distinction 'between the *form* of theological thought and its *content*' (Yerkes 1983 p.173). Hegel, that is to say, wishes to continue in some way to hold to the teaching enshrined in the Christian tradition, but to do so in language appropriately modified to suit the requirements of modern rationality. Rationalist though he is, however, Hegel by no means produces the straightforward reduction of language of the kind that is the mark of some recent works of theology. His treatment of the atonement continues to employ much of the language of theology before the

Enlightenment – its *form* - and therefore cannot be said to have abandoned the content entirely. There are, moreover, many places which contain more than mere echoes of traditional concerns. Hegel realises that at the heart of the matter is the removal of opposition and estrangement between God and humankind (Hegel 1895 II p.347 and III p.67). He also follows Kant and Schleiermacher in rejecting a Manichaean account of evil. Accordingly he holds that because the world is not evil in itself the estrangement is an intrusion into the order of things, and therefore that reconciliation is the removal of a breach that ought not to be. He asks, also, as one thinking somewhere in the Lutheran tradition would be expected to do, whether reconciliation might be achieved by the subject 'through its own piety and devoutness'; at least appreciating the point of the question, even though his answer is at best equivocal (III pp.67ff). Hegel is also aware that evil is one of the dimensions of the topic that must be taken into account.

But it is there that the rift between form and content begins to appear. There is always in Hegel a tendency to treat evil as part of the order of things, a necessary if negative stage in the emergence of rationally self-aware beings. The idea that it is something totally hostile to the good creation that must be overcome is foreign to the spirit of Hegel's work, although it has nearly always been a working assumption of classical Christian theology. He even distances himself from the moral realism of Kant's philosophy in the use he makes of one of the traditional metaphors of atonement, that of victory. 'The battle is past, and Man is conscious that it is not a case of battle, as it is in... the Kantian Philosophy, in which Evil is indeed to be overcome, but in which it confronts the Good in virtue of its own essential nature, and in which infinite progress is what is highest of all' (III pp.129f). Against such an interpretation it

19

will be argued below that we do not understand the ministry and death of Jesus unless we construe them as a real battle with the evil that afflicts the creation. In the passage from Hegel, by contrast, there are the seeds of modern progressive optimism and a virtual ignoring of the gross evil that put Jesus on the cross.

Hegel's reduction of the victory theme is one symptom of the fact that despite survivals of Christian conceptuality in his philosophy, the forms have for the most part been filled with foreign content. The chief reason is that the moral and affective dimensions of the content have been all but overwhelmed by the intellectual. For Paul, reconciliation meant, among other things, the restoration, achieved at the cost of the life of the Son of God, of a broken relationship between the eternal God and his erring creatures. For Hegel the theology of the cross as the historical place where the demonic corruption of the goodness of the created order is met by the holy love of God melts into the background, giving way to a merely formal statement of the incarnation and that in turn to an even more formal statement of the philosophical teaching that, according to him, the doctrine of the incarnation is meant to incapsulate. What was to do with the mending of broken relationships becomes in effect the solution of a philosophical puzzle: how may the finite and the infinite be thought together? The moral question is intellectualized, reduced to an epistemological one.

The way in which this happens is different from the treatment in Schleiermacher. There it is the penal aspects which become residual; in Hegel they are in effect ignored, and the focus of interest shifts from the cross to the incarnation. But that, too, is interpreted to mean something other than it has traditionally been supposed to say. Once divorced from the classical doctrine of the atonement it, too, comes to be treated more in intellectual than in broader human terms. Speaking of 'reconciliation, truth, freedom' Hegel says that 'The main idea which in a popular form expresses the truth, is that of the unity of the divine and human natures; God has become Man' (II p.347). Hegel's chief interest is in the philosophical generalisation that can be extracted from such a claim, and that is one in which both incarnation and atonement are made to mean the same. Both teach the removal of an opposition, but it is not the opposition between holy God and sinful man so much as that between the philosophical infinite and finite. 'Reconciliation' comes to mean little more than the process of so thinking together God and the human mind that they are understood to be at base one and the same. It is not quite fair to say that Hegel makes the doctrine of reconciliation simply the solution of a philosophical puzzle of how two orders of being, often supposed to be contraries of each other, are to be thought in relation with each other. From one point of view, his is as much a moral concern as that of the orthodox Christian tradition. In particular, he wished to restore the unity of culture that had been lost as the result of both modern criticism and the modern form of piety which, with its stress on the otherness of God and the utter insignificance of the moral agent, crushed the believer under a sense of the distance of the deity. Hegel was concerned with reconciliation in the sense that he wanted to restore a genuine Christianity, oriented to human well-being and the good ordering of society. But in the process of his attempted restoration, much of the content of the Christian tradition's teaching about salvation came to be lost. Gone was the orientation of the doctrine to matters of cosmic and human evil, as well as to the historical cross of Jesus as the place where they are met and overcome.

The problems reveal themselves most clearly in the well-known terms of Hegel's treatment of Christianity, *Begriff* (concept) and *Vorstellung* (representation). The meaning of these central concepts has been discussed in a number of recent studies (Fackenheim 1967, Yerkes 1983), and need not be repeated in detail here, particularly as we are chiefly concerned to understand what happens with their help to the traditional doctrines. The chief point to be made by means of the distinction between the two terms is that particular religious systems, based as they are on specific persons and events, are necessarily expressed in terms of *Vorstellungen*, which, because they rely on imagination and representation are unable to make their doctrines fully universal. Even Christianity, the 'absolute religion', falls short, in its historical form, of the clarity and certainty that philosophy requires, so that its doctrines have to be elevated and transmuted into more adequate conceptual form (the *Begriff*). In theory, the concept maintains the elements of truth contained in the representation, intended as it is to demonstrate the universal truth inherent within the particular religion. Hegel's intention is to be loyal to the *content* of Christianity. But his rational drive is too strong. The very fact that pure philosophical conceptuality is presumed to be 'higher' than a form of theology still dependent on imaginative or pictorial representation betrays the essential rationalism of the undertaking. The underlying approach is still that utterly clear and distinct ideas are more suited to tell the way things are than that language which draws upon sense, imagination and the historically particular.

Hegel, like Kant and Schleiermacher, asks questions which have to be faced. If Christian theology is to make universal claims about human life in the world, it must provide some account of the intellectual status of the language it uses. Pictures and images do not obviously point beyond themselves in such a way that they convey theological content, particularly when that content affects to mediate the being and action of God. Hegel's attempted rational account of Christianity, however, appears to deny aspects of the tradition which have made Christianity what it is. He therefore presents us with a real choice. Christian claims appear to depend on some direct relation to the story that is told of Jesus of Nazareth, narrated as it is in language containing 'pictorial', representational elements. That is particularly true of the metaphors in which the doctrine of the atonement has been spelled out, but it would seem that, on an account like Hegel's, they are at best of secondary value, serving only as provisional ways to express what must be put better in other words. If, then, the old forms of expression are to be retained, it must be shown that they are more rather than less suitable ways in which to express the truth of the Christian claim.

V   Rationalism and Rationality

It does not require wide reading in recent theology to realise that all the types of rationalism outlined above are with us still, often in cruder form. They are the reason why we find it difficult to hear what the Bible and theology before the Enlightenment are saying to us, let alone to be convinced by them. In that respect, Kant, Schleiermacher and Hegel are important because they are the presiding geniuses of the age. And genius is the word, for they have all marked our intellectual times indelibly and cannot be evaded by simply ignoring or going behind them. Rather, an attempt must be made to go beyond and to some extent against them. A programme designed to do so will have two sides, arguments against rationalism and a demonstration that an alternative approach is possible. Yet there is a limit to what can be done by argument alone. From one point of view, our three rationalists only recognise what is there. As another, and equally important nineteenth century thinker,

Kierkegaard, pointed out, authentic Christianity is intrinsically offensive. Its very particularity, and even more its centring of doctrines of God and salvation on the figure of a crucified teacher in such a way that the teacher becomes the teaching, is an offence to the intellect and moral sense of the 'natural' person. Kierkegaard is right in his central claim that in certain essential respects the contemporary of Jesus has no advantages over those of us who live two thousand years later. It offended then (see e.g. 1 Cor. 1f) as it does now that God should come to speech not as a philosophical teaching but through a man executed for blasphemy and sedition. It offends the moral sense also that human redemption should come as sheer gift in so unattractive a packaging.

Such claims offend not only our rationalism but also other aspects of our human response to the world. Yet that is not the same as to say that there is no good reason for believing them. One implication of the Christian gospel is that in its light the true nature of the human condition is revealed and, indeed, realised. Even those like Paul and Kierkegaard who have been most insistent on the offence and apparent absurdity of the cross have at the same time argued for its meaning and truth. They have not denied that the offence requires explanation and interpretation. In that respect the three thinkers whose views have been used as instances of mistranslations of the tradition were attempting a necessary task. All sought to be true to the meaning of their subject. What is being questioned is the adequacy of the assumptions with which they approached their task.

The aim of this book, accordingly, is to reappropriate aspects of the Christian tradition which rationalist criticism has called radically into question. The integrity of Christian faith, worship and life demands that the legacy of the past be assessed more positively than in the essays we have surveyed. Yet, as has already been argued, we cannot ignore the questions they ask of the language of the Bible and the tradition. One encouragement in the enterprise is that thinkers in many other disciplines are often more aware than theologians of the weaknesses of rationalism. During and since the Enlightenment there has been an alternative tradition which has refused to accept the dogmas of the age. As those dogmas come increasingly into question, that tradition is coming to the surface like a stream long underground. In the next chapter, accordingly, I shall centre attention on the question of the nature of metaphor and by that means draw from that stream some of its waters. In that way, an approach to the interpretation of the doctrine of the atonement different from those of Kant, Schleiermacher, Hegel and their successors will be essayed. The aim will be to find a rationality which, because it is not rationalist, has better claim to express the truth of the doctrine without detracting from the historical concreteness and fathomless depths of its object: specifically, to show that metaphor is both a pervasive feature of our language and that it is a way of telling things as they are. Once that has been done, we shall be in a position to examine, in three succeeding chapters, some of the central metaphors of atonement, in which the story of Jesus is seen to depict a victory, an act of justice and a sacrifice.

2

Metaphor and Theological Language

> It is among the miseries of the present age that it recognises no medium between *Literal* and *Metaphorical*. Faith is either to be buried in the dead letter, or its name and honours usurped by a counterfeit product of the mechanical understanding.
>
> *Samuel Taylor Coleridge*

I The Dynamics of Metaphor

Coleridge's words reveal his customary sharpness of perception, although his words also make an assumption which this chapter is designed to contest: that metaphor is at best of secondary value for the expression of truth and is a term of art rather than a tool of reason (in Hegelian terms a representation rather than a concept). But if there is one thing that is becoming increasingly apparent, it is that such a view is at best a simplification, at worst an intellectually disastrous misunderstanding of language and how it works. Much has been written on the topic in recent years, and in this chapter some of the leading works will be quarried in order to develop an account of the kind of thing that metaphors are and do. The programme will be to extract certain major discoveries from the literature, in order to show how they help us to reappropriate Christian teaching about the atonement.

It is not easy to offer a satisfactory definition of metaphor, as is evident from the fact that Ingolf Dalferth (1981 p.218) can cite a book, published in 1964 when the current debate had scarcely begun, which listed 125 definitions. In any case, the whole burden of this chapter is that metaphor is such a pervasive feature of our language that any tight definition would very likely exclude many respectable instances. Nothing therefore is to be gained from attempting to decide the matter in advance. If it is hoped to show that a particular family of metaphors opens windows on reality for those who order their thinking and life with its help, the first requirement is to show how the language works. The proof of the pudding will be in the eating; and a demonstration of how the words work as part of the Christian theological enterprise will be more persuasive than fitting them into some theoretical scheme decided in advance. What we need rather is a working definition, something that will enable the exploration to begin, and this is provided by Aristotle's classic definition of metaphor as 'the application of an alien name by transference' (*Poetics* 1457 b7-8).

The definition simply points us to what happens in some uses of language: a term belonging somewhere else is used in an unusual context, as when an assurance is described as copper-bottomed or the death of a man on a cross as a victory. Once we ask further questions of Aristotle, complexities rapidly begin to appear. What does he mean by 'name'? Is metaphorical meaning to be found in single words, or can it be understood only in the context of whole or part sentences? There are many debates about this and other similar points, but at this stage I want to concentrate on one point, namely the notion that metaphor involves the transfer of a word or words from one context to another. It is something done to and with language, as Nelson Goodman has suggested in a number of expressions, which, it will be noted, are themselves highly metaphorical. Metaphor, he says, is 'teaching an old word new tricks', 'a calculated category mistake', 'an affair between a predicate with a past and an object that yields while protesting' (Goodman 1969 pp.68,73,69). The common feature that makes a metaphor a metaphor is that words come to be used in a new or unusual way in human speech.

According, however, to the tradition we encountered in the previous chapter, that is precisely what is wrong with metaphor. It is not so much a use as a *misuse* of language, because it offends against rationalist canons of meaning. On such an account, truth-telling can be achieved only in language which is utterly clear and distinct. Metaphor blurs the edges, and is therefore inherently suspect. Hobbes was one philosopher explicitly to list metaphor among the abuses of language, listing the occasions 'when (men) use words metaphorically; that is, in other sense than that they are ordained for; and thereby deceive others' (Hobbes 1651/1962 p.34). Notice, however, that Hobbes's statement assumes that there is a proper use of language. Words are 'ordained' – by whom? Is not that a metaphor? – for precise literal use; anything else serves for 'deceit'. Judged by such a standard, any word usage that involves change must be distrusted as an abuse. It may perhaps be useful as ornament, dressing up the truth pleasantly, but is more likely to betray it.

The view of metaphor as an abuse of language came, like other rationalist beliefs, to its climax in the Age of Reason, but has a long history, which has been traced back to other remarks of Aristotle on the subject (Ricoeur 1977 pp.44ff). One effect has been to consign metaphor to the realm of rhetoric, which has itself increasingly come into question as a discipline concerned more with 'deceit' than with respectable forms of persuasion (Boothe 1974). Thus we may describe a speech as *mere* rhetoric, just as a word is sometimes held to be a *mere* metaphor. We are back in the realm of first and second class types of discourse. An absolute division, accordingly, came to be made between

29

argument and rhetoric, truth and ornament, literal and metaphorical, with all the virtues on one side, all the vices on the other. The outcome was a belief that what cannot be translated from metaphorical into 'literal' language cannot be held to be true. On such an account, metaphor is disqualified from being a means of our rational interaction with the world: *unless it ceases to be metaphor, it cannot tell the truth.*

Recent writers, however, are almost unanimous in rejecting the old view, although there is, hardly surprisingly, less agreement about the way in which a more positive doctrine should be developed. Highly significant here is the fact that recent work gives much attention to the place of metaphor in scientific discovery, the one sphere in which, on the rationalist account, we should not expect to find it. The fact is, however, that it is now widely held that metaphor plays an essential part. Two main approaches to the topic can be found in recent philosophy. Both hold, in distinction from the old view, that no advance in knowledge of the world is possible without changes in the meaning of words, that is to say, by means of the development of metaphors or other figures of speech. Classical physics, for example, developed with the help of the metaphorical description of the universe as a machine, as the words of Descartes suggest: 'I have described the Earth and the whole visible universe *as if it were* a machine' (cited by Turbayne 1970 p.39). Advances beyond classical physics took place partly with the help of another metaphor, which has itself since developed a precise technical meaning, the notion of a *field*.

The distinction between the two different approaches concerns the ways in which they conceive the linguistic change to take place. Ingolf Dalferth argues that the use of a metaphor precedes the making of new discoveries by, so to speak, providing the linguistic equipment with the help of which the nature of the world may be better understood (Dalferth 1981 pp.230-5). We first make our spade, and then we dig. Both the *machine* and *field* examples might illustrate the process: someone thinks that *machine* is a good word to try, and with its help succeeds in advancing the subject. The weakness of the view is that it makes too rigid a distinction between what we do as users of language and as discoverers of features of our world. The second interpretation, by contrast, sees a closer relation between language and discovery. It is not that metaphor *precedes* discovery, helping to make it possible, but rather that new language and discovery happen together, with metaphor serving as the *vehicle* of discovery. Such a view is argued by Richard Boyd, who holds that metaphors are a way of obtaining what he calls 'epistemic access' to the world. We comprehend aspects of the world as we find the new words to use in our search for understanding. Metaphor, therefore, is not simply a preliminary tool to be discarded when a better way of saying things is found, but 'one of the many devices available to the scientific community... to accomplish the task of *accommodation of language to the causal structure of the world*' (Boyd 1979 p.358). The last words, 'accommodation of language to the causal structure of the world', are of supreme importance. Language, to speak about the world, must become, so to speak, 'world-shaped'. It follows that if it is to be the means of articulating what was not known before, it must change. That is how we gain 'epistemic access': being enabled by language to 'cut the world at its joints', to use another of Boyd's ways of putting it.

The belief that language changes as we understand our world more and so that we may understand it better has a number of implications. The first is that the scientist as much as the artist is required to use the imagination as much as sense and reason in advancing the discipline. We are not disembodied intellects, but require the harmony of sense and reason which only imagination can supply.[1] In the scientific use of metaphor the creation of the imagination – that is to say, a concrete image drawn from one part of human experience of the world and transferred to a new context – becomes the means of expressing truth about the way the world is. Such a theory of language is the opposite of that outlined in Chapter 1, Section IV above, that the only way of penetrating to the real truth is by purifying our concepts of all imaginative and representative content. The second implication is that we are liberated from some of the more simplistic views of the scientist's relation to nature which, we may realise, is not one of merely intellectual or technological dominance, but consists of an interaction, a dynamic process, in which language is moulded to reality as different features of the world are revealed with its assistance. Overall, accordingly, the general lesson to be learned is that metaphors are not odd, unusual, improper or merely decorative. They are so pervasive a part of our experience that they are a, if not *the*, clue to what language is and does.

II   *Words and the World*

Examples taken from recent writing in the philosophy of science have dominated the argument so far for obvious reasons. The sciences have become for our culture the models of reliable knowledge of our world. If metaphor is necessary there, it cannot be dismissed as an abuse of language; and if it cannot, we must consider what follows for our understanding of the way language works and the kind of world we live in. So far as language is concerned, we are liberated from the narrow view that the only words

1. For a discussion, owing much to Coleridge, of the importance of the imagination in a related context, see my *Enlightenment and Alienation* (1985) pp.30ff.

capable of being true are those which in some way directly 'fit' the world as a mirror image fits a face; that some words – supposedly 'literal' ones – directly reflect reality while others entirely or mostly fail to do so. The most notable conversion away from the mirroring view of language in recent times is to be seen in Wittgenstein's pilgrimage from the *Tractatus* (1921) to the *Philosophical Investigations* (1945-9). But as the debate about what Wittgenstein's new understanding of meaning has shown, his discoveries about the elusiveness of the relation of language and the world can be taken in a number of ways. On the one hand, they can be taken to suggest that because there is no direct correspondence between words and things no satisfactory account can be given of such relation as there is. Words are all we have, so that our supposed 'discoveries' are no more than our imposing of mental constructs upon an essentially unknown world. Some theories of theological language and metaphor have tended in this direction (Soskice 1985, pp.103ff). The implausibility of an attempt to account for *all* language in that way is suggested by the fact that the sciences do appear to have advanced our knowledge of what the world actually is. Nevertheless, it is a doctrine that will continue to find advocates simply because it is so difficult to give a finally satisfactory account of the way words do 'fit' the world. We may compare with it Nietszche's view, with which Jüngel begins his discussion of metaphor, that because claims for truth have an irreducibly metaphorical structure there can be no truth (Jüngel 1974 p.82).

On the other hand, the disappearance of the conception of language as a mirror of reality can be taken as an opportunity to develop an alternative 'realist' account to the traditional one. It can be argued that the fact that there does appear to be a cutting of the world at its joints by means of metaphor requires a different theory of the relation of words and things. The more sceptical account, it may be argued, is attractive only because it asks too much, demanding in a rationalist manner a complete and exhaustive account of the fit between words and the world. But that is to beg the whole question of what we are to expect of our language. As finite beings, we should more modestly demand only partial and provisional success with our naming and describing: 'we know in part.' The strength of the account of metaphor being developed here is that it is consistent with that more modest requirement. Metaphor claims only an indirect purchase on reality, bringing to expression some but not all aspects and relationships of the segment of the world to which it is directed. As a very simple example of the way it works, we may take the word *muscle*, which when first used presumably drew upon some of the associations of the Latin *musculus*, 'little mouse'. No-one now thinks of those associations, but that is because it has been so successful. When it first emerged as a metaphor it succeeded precisely because in an indirect way it enabled physiologists to name and begin to understand one part of the anatomy.

The example is also useful as an introduction to another very important feature of the topic, and one which is the cause of much confusion. What is the difference between a metaphorical and a literal use of a term? As we have seen, it was once widely believed that that if there is to be genuine knowledge, it must be expressed in literal terms, any metaphors having first been appropriately 'translated'. Such a doctrine presupposes something that the argument so far has been seeking to undermine, that certain privileged words directly correspond to things, while others do not. Yet if the relation between words and things is essentially indirect, part of a process of interaction between person and world, that static view has to disappear. There are no words that are 'literal' in all times and places, nor can words be neatly divided into two classes in that way. The same word can begin life as a metaphor and become a literal usage, as the example of *muscle* shows. It also shows, however, that there is a difference between the literal and the metaphorical. In process of time, the metaphorical becomes literal. What then is the difference? Not that it now mirrors its object as once it did not, but that it has come to be accepted as the primary use of the term (Ricoeur 1977 p.291). *The difference between literal and metaphorical is a difference between different ways of using a word in discourse.*

One implication of that claim is that there can be no absolute distinction between the literal and the metaphorical because the same word is sometimes one, sometimes the other. We can conceive of some technical terms which have lost almost all of their metaphorical characteristics – though we may still ask, for example, how far this is completely true of *field* in *magnetic field* – while others, for example *eternal generation*, retain more of them. It is always a matter of observing how a word is used in its context. Language is dynamic and protean, and words cannot be sorted into mutually exclusive classes. And so metaphors die, but may also be recalled to life, and over a period of time reveal a wide spectrum of movement to and from the metaphorical. The important point for our purposes is that the truth of a claim about the world does not depend upon whether it is expressed in literal or metaphorical terms, but upon whether language of whatever kind expresses human interaction with reality successfully (truthfully) or not. The question of how we may be able to tell whether a metaphor is truthful or not will exercise us in the course of the book. The main point here is to reinforce the conclusion of the previous section. There it was claimed that metaphor is a pervasive feature of language. Here the contention is that, despite the fact that it does remain possible to claim that metaphor can be interpreted in a purely subjective way – speaking primarily of *our* minds and *our* usage, not of the world outside – a more plausible account is that it is the way by which we are enabled to speak about the real world. If that is so, what kind of world is it with which we have to do?

III   Words and the **World**

The previous sections have been devoted chiefly to words, how they work, change and inform. It was not possible, however, to speak about language without encroaching on the matter of reality. The two enquiries, about words and things, are so closely intertwined that they cannot be completely abstracted from each other. In this section, the emphasis will change from the words to the things, in an examination of the implications the discoveries about language have for our understanding of the world. I begin with a letter written by Coleridge in 1800 (cited by Stanford 1936 pp.16f):

> Is *thinking* impossible without arbitrary signs? And how far is the word 'arbitrary' a misnomer? Are not words, etc., part and germinations of the plant? ... In something of this sort I would endeavour to destroy the old antithesis *of Words* and *Things:* elevating, as it were words into Things and living Things, too.

The crucial move made by Coleridge in that passage is the placing of quotation marks around the word *arbitrary*. He is suggesting that it is wrong to suppose that words are simply arbitrary signs and symbols. At one level, they undoubtedly are. To call something *a cow* rather than *une vache* depends almost entirely on factors independent of the relation of language and reality. But that is not the level at which Coleridge is speaking and at which language is philosophically interesting. The interesting question is: given that we call a cow a cow, what is language doing in using the term in discourse about the world? What does the successful use of language tell us about the nature of the world we live in? The argument so far has been designed to suggest that words function, in natural science for example, as part of human interaction with nature. They are, as Michael Polanyi has taught us, the articulate level of our many-faceted relationship with the world about us, perhaps the highest feature of our indwelling of our environment.

To realise some of the implications of the argument so far, we turn from scientific to literary uses of metaphor. Here the most illuminating remarks are to be found in a book written by a classical scholar half a century ago. The interest of W.B. Stanford's *Greek Metaphor* lies in the move he makes from the logic of metaphor to its ontological implications. The logic of the matter, as he sees it, is that in metaphor patterns of meaning are created from the fusion of notions which are, and remain, disparate. A little mouse is one thing, a muscle quite another; and yet knowledge is created by their fusion. That is not, however, a merely linguistic matter, for the fact that things happen in such a way tells us something of the world we live in. It demonstrates, we can say following Coleridge, the way in which words are things and things words. Stanford appeals to the view of S.J. Brown that 'imagery is a witness to the harmony between mind and matter' (p.99). Metaphor is a supreme instance of the harmony that can be attained between language and the world. Therefore: the world is the kind of thing that can be interpreted in language. It is, or has – metaphorically! – a kind of language.

The key to the relation between language and world is something we have met already, its *indirectness*. The world can be known only indirectly, and therefore metaphor, being indirect, is the most appropriate form that a duly humble and listening language should take. In all this, there is a combination of openness and mystery, speech and silence, which makes the clarity and distinctness aimed at by the rationalist tradition positively hostile to the truth. Thus the tables are turned: metaphor, rather than being the cinderella of cognitive language, becomes the most, rather than the least, appropriate means of expressing the truth. If, then, we are to be true to the way things are in our world we must see metaphor as the most, not the least, significant part of our language. And so it is not at all fanciful to conceive our interaction with the world as a kind of conversation, in which, as in other conversations, there can be exploitation, misunderstanding and deliberate deafness, but, equally, the excitement of successful communication and discovery. It is not, of course, a conversation between equals, and the rather anthropomorphic language should be carefully qualified. But there is, none the less, much to be learned from Jüngel's characterisation of metaphor as the '*Geschehen von Wahrheit* (the taking place of truth)' (Jüngel 1974 p.107, his italics) in which there is a '*Wechselspiel* of man and the world, in which man understands himself cosmomorphically and the world anthropomorphically' (p.121). Because the world is, so to speak, our shape and we are world-shaped, there is a readiness of the world for our language, a community of world and person which enables the world to come to speech.

The relevance of such claims for the matter of Chapter 1 should now be evident. Rationalism represents an approach to language which attempts to find a more direct relation between mind and world than that suggested here. It wants to find privileged types of words and ways of discovery which give direct access to reality and are, at least in principle, immune from error. The result is that too much is attributed to mental operations and concepts, too little to the interaction of world, bodily sense and reason that is required by the more indirect relationship revealed by attention to the central place that metaphor plays in our conversation with our world. Rationalism is congenitally suspicious of imagination; by contrast, the argument here is that it is an essential part of our openness to the world. To this, the rationalist will reply that it is the source of all kind of lies, deceptions and pure invention. A rejoinder will not deny the claim, but contend that the same is true of all our faculties, operating as they do under the conditions of finitude and sin. There is nothing godlike about the reason that elevates it above other human faculties, for it is the source of demonic pride as much as of illumination. All our intellectual, aesthetic and moral endeavours fail unless they take place in due repentance and subordination to the truth.

The conclusion, accordingly, is that simply in virtue of the greater modesty of its claims for comprehension, metaphor is a primary vehicle of human rationality and superior to the pure concept (if such exists, as must be doubtful). It is therefore a mark of Aristotle's own genius that he made the observation – though in a slightly different context – that to create good metaphors is a mark of genius (*Poetics* 1459 a7). To make and to express in language discoveries about our world requires an openness and receptivity that in most cases must amount to genius. The world gives up its secrets but not predictably or to order, as the history of science and culture alike reveal. We must, therefore, treasure our metaphors, particularly those which have, over the centuries, commended themselves as especially illuminating in the human quest to come to terms with the meaning of our universe and of our life in it; while not forgetting that those which have lost metaphorical status have often done so precisely because of their once successful use as metaphors.

IV   Metaphor in Theology

The argument of the previous sections was developed with the help of some approaches, broadly describable as 'realist', to the philosophy of science. It was claimed that metaphor is one of the ways, perhaps *the* way, in which the world as it exists 'outside' the mind of the observer is discovered and understood. The account would undoubtedly be contested by those who would take a more idealist approach to the theory of knowledge, asking whether we can transcend the inbuilt structures of our minds and senses. In defence of the position being developed here two points can be made. The first is that it is generally in line with a widespread movement, charted for example by Richard Bernstein (1985), beyond the kind of terms in which epistemology has been discussed since Descartes. Many philosophers are rejecting the old choices between, for example, objectivism and relativism, and realising that the question has to be put in an entirely different way. The second is that although it is unlikely that a final solution to the problem will be found by argument alone, evidence in favour of the development will be provided if metaphor can be shown in practice to work in the way that has been outlined. The remainder of this book is designed to offer such a demonstration of language in action. At this stage the claim is to have given an attractive and plausible rationale of our human interaction with the world in language and, equally important, to have avoided the necessity of choice between narrowly 'objectivist' and 'subjectivist' epistemologies. That is not to deny, however, that a choice of some kind is required, for it must be true that, finally, we are either talking about something beyond the structures of the human mind or we are not. We may see the world through such structures and with their assistance, but unless it is *the world* we see, our position is finally completely subjectivist or even solipsist.

In her recent study of metaphor and its use in theology (to which the reader is recommended for the technical background to many of the points treated summarily in this chapter), Janet Martin Soskice has alluded to the fact that many theologians working in this area present a confused picture. Drawing on recent philosophy, they begin by advocating a realist use of metaphor and other symbols – in science, for example – but end by collapsing into subjectivism when they come to theology (Soskice 1985 p.105).[2] Why should this be so? The first reason, or rather cluster of reasons, derives from theology's continuing captivity to Kantian theories of knowledge. It is widely supposed that our descriptive words speak only of the phenomenal world, the world, that is, which is presented to our senses. Anything beyond that is 'subjective.' Another way of putting it would be to say that although empiricism has been discredited in much science and philosophy, it still casts its spell upon the theologians. Both Kantianism and empiricism, however, are built upon a narrow view of the way language relates to reality; that, precisely, which modern studies of metaphor appear to have destroyed. It is not only the owl of Minerva which takes flight after dusk. But if theories which distinguish rigidly between different types of discourse continue to affect approaches to theology, it can scarcely be surprising that theological language should appear to be not about the real world, but about the human response to reality or the structures of our minds.

2. An instance is McFague (1983). The chief systematic weakness of the book is that it combines a wide knowledge of recent developments with a continued dependence upon an old theory of meaning, that is, that 'literal' language is language that 'mirrors' reality. A collapse into idealism is inevitable.

Of a piece with a continuing captivity to fading epistemologies is a tendency for modern theologies to be dominated by literary uses of metaphor. As we have seen in the case of the claim that 'imagery is a witness to the harmony between mind and matter' (above p.37), such appeal is not necessarily 'subjectivist'. But a preoccupation with literary rather than scientific uses of metaphor can lead to a conception of – for example – biblical metaphors as imaginative expressions of human experience of the world rather than as means by which we speak about the reality of God. That is not to deny that much is to be learned about the nature of theological language from literary studies, especially, perhaps, those concerned with the nature of narrative (see Frei 1974). Indeed, the theological language at the heart of this study belongs in narrative, for to describe Jesus' life, death and resurrection as a victory or sacrifice is to use those words of the narrative in such a way that part of the meaning of the whole might be understood. In other words, the metaphors are the means by which it is possible to speak of the meaning of the gospel narratives taken as a whole. But it by no means follows that another feature the narratives share with some forms of literature is that they are largely free human inventions, vaguely grounded in what happened in Palestine in the first century of our era.

The second reason for the widespread collapse of theology into idealism is a better one, though, it is to be hoped, one that is not finally convincing. Theological language is necessarily different from and more difficult than the language of science because God, however he be conceived, is related to the human mind in a different way from the things we call the natural universe. It might therefore be suggested that while 'realism' is the appropriate way to approach the knowledge of the one realm, 'idealism' or some form of subjectivism is more appropriate when the boundary is crossed into the other. The difficulty of avoiding such a development is made greater by the way in which contemporary theology is often done. Beginning with the supposedly known world – though the discussion of metaphor in science would suggest that the fact of its being known is not always as straightforward as some accounts suggest – an attempt is made to use language of the known to cross a gulf to a supposedly unknown God. The stress falls not, as it does in the case of scientific language, on the creation of new language in conversation with the world, but on the projection by analogy of familiar terms on to the (supposedly) unfamiliar. It is scarcely surprising that a theological approach of this kind should fall prey to suspicions of *mere* projection, or that it should be supposed even by its users to function idealistically. Is it then possible to develop an account of theological metaphor which shows it to work in a *similar but distinctive* way in comparison with its use of the finite world?

Here we meet a problem which is complicated and philosophically controversial, but which must be faced in any discussion of theological language: the nature of reference. How, if at all, do we refer to God, and what is the status of such reference? We have reached here the crux of the matter of the realistic use of metaphor, because with the metaphors of atonement we propose to refer to the action of God by the use of words which are customarily used to refer to something else: *sacrifice* to the slaughter of an animal on an altar, *victory* to the outcome of a military engagement. What then is reference? We begin with a brief and general account. In general, to refer is to fix something by means of language so that it may be recognised, described, examined, investigated, etc.: it is to use a word to *stand for* something (Geach 1987). Of great assistance here is the fact that some recent accounts of reference have moved away from empiricist theories of meaning. Such theories hold that before we can refer to something, we must identify it by means of a set of descriptions. To use John Locke's example, only when we have described a metal of a certain colour and weight may we refer to it as 'gold'. The problems facing any attempted reference to God are on such a doctrine almost insuperable, certainly on an empiricist account, for they involve finding a set of descriptions for God before any reference can be made to the very action in the world by which we wish to identify him.

However, the empiricist account has, along with all empiricism, recently come under strong attack, as reversing what actually happens in reference. Saul Kripke, for example, has vigorously attacked the doctrine that reference is determined by means of descriptions, linguistic formulae which fix the reference of an entity because they are supposed to constitute its primary properties (Kripke 1980). Kripke's argument is to the effect that the essential properties of an entity are only discoverable *after* reference has been made, and so necessarily cannot be the means of fixing reference. Reference may be fixed *with the aid of* certain properties – for example, the colour and weight of gold – but the reference itself is usually first made by ostension or 'baptism', as a result of which a certain kind of metal comes to be given a particular name by a certain community of speakers (in this case the users of English). The important point is that reference has to to do with picking something out of the world: it is the way in which we deal, by means of language, with things:

> It is in general not the case that the reference of a name is determined by some uniquely identifying marks... (E)ven if in some special cases... a reference *is* determined by a description, by some uniquely identifying

property, what that property is doing in many cases of designation is not giving a synonym...; it is, rather, fixing a reference. (p.106)

Once reference has been fixed, science may set out on its attempt to find what is true of the real world – 'the nature, and thus the essence (in the philosophical sense) of the kind' (p.138).

In the important paper to which reference has already been made, Richard Boyd (1979) has shown how metaphor takes its place in such a process of fixing reference. If we fix the meaning of something metaphorically – by referring to the cross as a sacrifice or a part of the anatomy as muscle – we do two things. First, we use a word which points to part of the world in such a way that we can begin to talk and think about it. Second, in the process we enable the meaning of the language to change as it is adapted to those features of the world which we hope it will help us to understand, what Boyd calls accommodating to the causal structure of the world. When we open ourselves to the world with the help of the language, the world – if we have found the right metaphor[3] – will enforce, so to speak, changes in the meaning of the words we use. Metaphor thus makes possible a dual process, of discovery and the development of our language better to speak about its object. 'This sort of linguistically mediated epistemic success... is the very core of reference' (Boyd pp. 398f).

3. The 'if' is, without doubt, of gigantic proportions. Decisions about the 'rightness' of a metaphor will involve verification processes of great complexity, among them questions about the place of words in the forms of life in which they operate. From the very nature of the case there can, because there is no direct mirroring of the world, be nothing of the kind attempted in old-fashioned verificationism. The whole of this book can be seen as one aspect of a many sided process in which traditional Christian metaphors are being tested for rightness.

Theological language is not concerned to accommodate language to causal features of the world after the manner of natural science. But in so far as the first Christians can be said – metaphorically – to have found themselves, after what had happened with Jesus, newly accommodated to 'the causal structures of reality' – set in a different place before God and in the world – the language they used of the atonement can be understood in a similar way. The central focus of the proclamation after Easter was that the events of Jesus' history, and particularly of the Easter period, had changed the status of believers, indeed of the whole world. The metaphors of atonement are ways of expressing the significance of what had happened and was happening. They therefore enable the Christian community to speak of God as he is found in concrete personal relationship with human beings and their world. Language that is customarily used of religious, legal, commercial and military relationships is used to identify a divine action towards the world in which God is actively present remaking broken relationships. That is a causal fixing of reference in the sense that reference is made to God by means of a narration of historical happenings and their outcome.

That, however, is not the end of the matter, as some conceptions of 'narrative theology' may appear to suggest, but the beginning. There can be no evasion of the further question of what follows from the fact that we refer to God and his actions by means of narratives summarised by a number of central metaphors. Unless some account is attempted of the relation of our language to the real world – and that is not the same as a quest for some neutral 'foundation' outside the language[4] – it may appear that we are *merely* telling stories. The primary way of our fixing the reference of *God* is, indeed, through the telling of the biblical narratives in the light of previous uses of them by the Christian community. But once reference has been fixed the theological task has scarcely begun. Are we justified in speaking of God in this way? In what sense, if any, is it possible to speak of God as he is in himself, apart from and as the basis of his articulation in narrative? (That is, of course, the question of the nature of God as triune.) Such systematic questions are imposed on the one who would wish to claim that the metaphors tell us the truth about where we really stand in the world.

To return, however, to the main theme of this chapter. Our concern has been with the degree to which human language is adequate to that which it seeks to express. We have seen that the metaphorical use of language is the heart of the way in which we come to speak of our world, approaching it as we do indirectly in the hope that by forcing changes in our language it will enable us to come to a measure of understanding of its structures. What is the case with our language of the world in general is even more characteristic of theological language. Because we are not able to speak of the action and being of God independently of the metaphors in which they are first expressed, we must begin with the language and move from there to a discussion of how the language has worked – or failed to work – and may still work as a way of articulating how the action of God may be conceived to take place here and now. Before, however, we move to the first main stage of the enquiry, some clarificatory points remain to be made.

4. Thus far, I wish to share in the critique of 'foundationalism' which is at present fashionable in Christian theology; see especially Thiemann 1985. But in so far as a denial of foundationalism is thought to entail the denial of an explicit epistemology, I wish to have nothing to do with it.

V   *Language in Action*

First: to discuss together the doctrine of the atonement and the nature of theological language brings considerable advantages. Many treatments of the matter of theological language discuss the nature of analogy, symbolism and metaphor at great length and in general, and then show how their work bears upon theological language. The outcome is a tendency to abstraction; for example, to yet more discussions of the meaning of the term *Father* when it is used of God (e.g. McFague 1983). Such abstraction carries the danger that certain expectations or presuppositions will be taken into the discussion and prevent the theological meaning from speaking for itself. By contrast, to begin with the concrete relationships expressed in the New Testament metaphors, is to centre attention on the way in which theological language actually has been used and, perhaps, should or may be used now.

Second, there is an overwhelming case for holding that traditional atonement metaphor is particularly well suited to show that language takes shape in a kind of conversation. We have seen that according to Boyd's account it is scarcely an exaggeration to say that the world forces new meanings upon words. Language is not just the tool of the user, to be employed at will, but a subtle instrument whose meaning is in part the gift of the (indwelt) world to which it seeks to refer. That is true in science, as we have seen: the world gives itself to be understood in the sense that its perceived and experimentally revealed structures demand of us changes in our language. Metaphor, as we have seen, is a major way in which those changes are achieved as our language is moulded to fit the causal structures of reality. *A fortiori* is this true of the relationship of human beings to God in the light of the atonement, whose very centre is the historical action of God for and among those who had placed themselves outside the covenant relationship. Our language is remoulded as we are. If the fact of atonement takes its shape from the initiative of God, to be true to it our language must take a metaphorical shape corresponding to the changes brought about by the incarnation, cross and resurrection of Jesus.

Third, however, it must not be supposed that certain images or forms of language are in some way forced upon the theologian by a bolt from the blue, in contradiction of all other experience. The biblical words upon which theology has drawn are themselves often metaphors, changes of language imposed upon the users by changes of personal situation and understanding. The language that is adopted already belongs in a context, and that context is not only a specific tradition – although it certainly is that – but the tradition as it makes variations on almost universal features of human thought and speculation. To take the example which will form the framework for a later chapter, Greeks and Hebrews alike had concepts of the justice or righteous-ness of God, because concern with the rights and wrongs of life on earth animated not only the prophets, priests and wise of Israel but also Greek philosophers and artists. Yet the way the concept was understood was particular to the traditions within which they lived and thought. Christian talk of the righteousness of God is shaped by that of Israel as it comes to a climax in the cross of Jesus.

George Steiner has made a similar point about the near universality of the currency of certain metaphors:

> We have histories of massacre and deception, but none of metaphor. We cannot accurately conceive what it must have been like to be the first to compare the colour of the sea with the dark of wine or to see autumn in a man's face. Such figures are new mappings of the

49

> world, they reorganise our habitation in reality. (Steiner
> 1975 p.23)

The last phrase is the central one for our purposes. The great
atonement metaphors, because they have articulated and
made real certain ways of inhabiting the world, continue to
have currency even where they have become debased or
dead metaphors (witness the many uses of *sacrifice* in
modern English). This may not be merely a matter of our
cultural heritage, but of the fact that they bring uniquely to
speech certain features of the human condition. Steiner
again:

> The quality of genius in the Greek and Hebrew
> statement of human possibility, the fact that no
> subsequent articulation of felt life in the Western
> tradition has been either as complete or formally
> inventive, are undeniable. (pp.21f)

The metaphors, therefore, belong in our culture because
they are historically important and because they have not
been superseded. But are they, in effect, dead metaphors,
dead not only because they have been domesticated but
because they no longer speak, no longer create space for
human living? That question remains the crucial one, even if
the rest of the argument so far has been accepted, and awaits
detailed treatment.

The fourth point is perhaps the most important theologically, and takes up a theme from earlier in the chapter. It was
there suggested that the creation of metaphorical language,
particularly in theology, is partly at least at the initiative of
that to which the language refers. If this is so, may it not be
that, far from the metaphors being mainly or simply
projections from standard to theological use, the reverse is
true, in the sense that the theological use operates nor-
matively and so alters the meaning of the word in its

everyday employment? In such a case, the new, metaphorical, meaning of the word would reflect light back on to the context from which the word was originally taken. That is not something that happens only in theology. Douglas Berggren has suggested that because metaphors operate, at least in part, by creating a tension between two ideas or subjects, the meaning of both terms may be transformed and yet preserved. For example: 'To construe life as a play or dream is not only to organise or interpret life in different ways, but also to give plays and dreams a significance that they might not otherwise have had' (Berggren 1962-3 p.243). That is to say, metaphor can have a revelatory function. Such an interpretation is particularly illuminating in theology, as Roger White has shown. There are, he argues, drawing on the thought of such diverse authorities as Plato, Aquinas, Barth and Wittgenstein, certain words in common use whose real and primary meaning is only revealed when we understand their use in theology. His example takes us very near to the idea that the atonement is a victory:

> For it is the whole of our Lord's ministry, and especially the Passion, that causes us to question where really is power and where really is impotence: is the apparently indisputable power of Pilate perhaps impotence, and the apparently indisputable acceptance of impotence by Jesus the only real power that can challenge the absoluteness of the constraints and conditions of this world which we treat as absolute and which hold us in their bondage? (White 1982 p.217)

Accordingly, when the New Testament speaks of the life, and particularly the cross, of Jesus as a sacrifice, a victory and the justification of the sinner, may it not be that we encounter not 'mere' metaphors but linguistic usages which demand a new way of thinking about and living in the world? Here is *real* sacrifice, victory and justice, so that what we thought the words meant is shown to be inadequate and in need of reshaping by that to which the language refers. And so our enquiry is established. In the next three chapters we shall look at three ways in which the story of Jesus can – or *must* – be understood to create ways both of speaking of God and of realising his action in the world. In each case, we shall ask whether they are viable ways of speaking about the life, death and resurrection of Jesus as redemption, atonement.

3

The Battlefield and the Demons

The first wrote, Wine is the strongest.
The second wrote, The king is strongest.
The third wrote, Women are strongest: but
above all things Truth beareth away the victory.
1 Esdras 3.10

I A Divine and Human Victory

The argument so far has charted two features of the modern
theological landscape. The first is the obstacles which some
recent ways of thought have placed before those who would
adopt traditional Christian conceptions of the atonement.
These obstacles must be faced and surmounted in any
serious attempt to appropriate the riches of the doctrine,
because they are not the product of prejudice alone but
derive in part from inadequate expression and embodiment
of Christian insight in the past. The second feature is more
positive: it is the increasing awareness that what have been
called modern ways of thought are not definitive, final or in
any way adequate to the variety and richness of the world
with which we have to do. Some recent explorations of the
way language develops in the course of human interaction
with the world give positive encouragement to the theologian, particularly in showing that not only the advance of
knowledge but also its very possibility depend upon the
extension of human language by metaphor and other
devices. The Christian church has always expressed its
understanding of redemption with the help of a number of
metaphors. We turn now to one of them.

About fifty years ago the Swedish theologian Gustav Aulén wrote his now famous study, *Christus Victor*, in which he claimed that the 'classic' way of conceiving the atonement was that in which Christ is viewed as the victor over the demonic forces holding human life in thrall. In the West, he held, the centrality of this theory had been lost because Tertullian and Cyprian, among others, had introduced into theology the notion of *satisfaction*. This both obscured the heart of the Christian message and paved the way for the critiques of Christianity by its opponents in the modern age (Aulén 1931/1970 pp.81f). The problem was what Aulén calls the Latin doctrine, which he claims to be legalistic, rationalistic and blind to the central teachings of the Fathers, which it rejects for inadequate reasons. Whether Aulén is justified in so wholesale a rejection of major aspects of the Western tradition must await treatment in a later chapter. Here we are concerned to examine his claim that, like the proponents of authentic early music, he has cleaned the generations' encrustations of dirt from a picture and laid bare the original in all its bright colours.

In *Christus Victor* Aulén gives two summary statements of what he calls the classic theory of the atonement. First:

> This type of view may be described provisionally as the 'dramatic'. Its central theme is the idea of the Atonement as a Divine conflict and victory; Christ – Christus Victor – fights against and triumphs over the evil powers of the world, the 'tyrants' under which mankind is in bondage and suffering, and in Him God reconciles the world to Himself. (p.4)

At the heart of this paragraph there lies a contrast between the atonement conceived as a transaction – for example, of a legal kind – and as a drama, in which something decisive happens to change the relations between God and humankind. It should also be noticed that there is a strong stress in

Aulén's account on the fact that it is a *divine* victory. In the second summary of the theory, a further point is made:

> God in Christ overcomes the hostile powers which hold man in bondage. At the same time, these hostile powers are also the executants of God's will. The patristic theology is dualistic, but it is not an absolute Dualism. The deliverance of man from the power of death and the devil is at the same time his deliverance from God's judgement. God is reconciled by His own act in reconciling the world to Himself. (p.59)

The pattern is clear. Aulén claims that, according to the classic theory, the cross of Christ is conceived – metaphorically, we might say – as a divine victory over certain powers of evil which are both evil and within divine control. Reconciliation is achieved because after the incarnation and death of Christ their power to do harm is taken away by God.

In view of the fact that Aulén considers the classic theory to be a satisfactory account not only of the doctrinal tradition but also of the biblical material, our first test must be of its conformity to the biblical teaching. And here it must be said that although there is support, it is not always as unambiguous as his confident account sometimes appears to suppose. A recent study has cast doubt upon the use made of Col. 2.15 (RSV: 'He disarmed the principalities and powers') by theologians such as Aulén, and suggested that the view that Christ met and defeated a host of cosmic enemies owes more to Origen than to the New Testament (Carr 1981 pp.168-71,176). The imagery of that text is almost certainly drawn from a Roman triumphal procession, but it is conceivable that the 'powers and authorities' are not Christ's opponents but the hosts of heaven cheering him on his way. Similarly, there is little explicit talk of victory elsewhere in Paul, while the Synoptic Gospels, though certainly using the language of struggle (see for example Mark 3.22-27) and the equally significant vocabulary of the kingdom of God, do not directly characterise the life and death of Jesus in language taken from the battlefield. That does not mean, of course, that it is wrong for us to see the gospel writers as depicting a kind of victory, but that must depend rather on the meaning they give to their narratives as a whole than on particular proof texts.

More direct help comes from the Johannine literature, and especially the book of Revelation, where it is the lamb bearing the marks of slaughter – a clear reference to the crucified and risen Jesus – who is confessed by the elders who stand round the throne of God: 'the Lion of the tribe of Judah... has conquered' (Rev.5.5f). The theme of victory is taken up later in that book, when the birth of the male child is interpreted by a description of a war in heaven in which Satan, in an echo of Luke 10.18 ('I saw Satan fall like lightning from heaven'), is thrown down from heaven to earth (Rev.12.7ff). Similarly, though without using military imagery, John's gospel depicts the progress of Jesus to the cross as a movement of victorious conquest, certainly if it is right to interpret 19.30 ('It is finished') in the light of 16.33 ('Be of good cheer, I have overcome the world') as a cry of triumph. It is from such a perspective that we may interpret the encounter with and defeat of evil that are so much a feature of the synoptic accounts of the ministry of Jesus. Whatever we make of the language of demons and demonic possession – and that will concern us later – it is clear that a kind of victory over forces which hold human life in bondage is being described. When Jesus speaks of a sick woman as a 'daughter of Abraham whom Satan bound for eighteen years' (Luke 13.16) it seems clear that he is depicting the enslavement of parts of the world to an evil which it is the calling of Jesus and his followers to destroy.

So far, then, there does appear to be biblical support for the general position that Aulén is advocating. It is possible to claim that in some authors the life and death of Jesus is understood as a victory. They are using a metaphor or set of metaphors – language drawn from one field of human activity – in order to expound the significance of the one about whom they are writing.

There are, however, distinctions to be made that appear to have been overlooked by Aulén. In particular, there are further dimensions of the story to be taken into account. The authors are not merely concerned with a divine act that is a past event, and certainly not with a merely cosmic conflict. The victory is both a continuing and an earthly one. Both sides must be stressed if we are to see the matter as more than a myth, a 'story of the gods'. In the first place, the victory of Christ is seen to continue in the life of the Christian, so that Paul can say that 'in all things we are conquerors through him who loved us' (Rom.8.37), while the Johannine authors conceive the victory as continuing in the life of the Christian community: 'For whatever is born of God overcomes the world; and this is the victory that overcomes the world, our faith' (1 John 5.4). Similarly, Rev.15.2 echoes the language we recently met in speaking of those, possibly the martyrs but perhaps more generally all Christian believers, who have conquered 'the beast'. In all this we are very much pointed forward to the theology of Irenaeus, whose concept of recapitulation enabled him to form a link between the way in which Jesus lived out the human story in a victorious way and the continuing of his victory in the life of the church. He is true to the insight of the New Testament writers that talk of a past victory is not to be isolated from matters of present practice.

The second dimension overlooked by Aulén is that the victory charted in the New Testament is as much human as divine. In this respect, the gospel narratives of the ministry of Jesus provide the essential framework for an understanding of the cross as a victory. A common criticism of Aulén's book is that it advocates too triumphalist a view of the atonement and fails to emphasise enough the human and even tragic elements of the story. Here, Dr. Carr's querying of the traditional interpretation of the Colossians passage will be of positive assistance if it points us to the life and cross of Jesus as the victory of the 'proper man' over human temptation and sin. Similarly, G.B. Caird's remark that the victory is achieved by obedience is illustrated by the progress of the narrative of Luke 4 (Caird 1956 pp.97ff). That chapter begins with the temptation of Jesus, which represents, so to speak, the opening engagement in a struggle destined to reach its culminating encounter in Gethsemane and on the cross (Luke 22.40-46 and 23.7). All the temptations are concerned in some way with the misuse of human power in relation to the created order, particularly as they might be conceived to present themselves to one claiming messiahship. In other words, they are in different ways conceived as temptations to idolatry, with worshipping 'the creature rather than the creator', in one of Paul's definitions of sin (Rom.1.25, cf 18). It is the refusal to succumb to the temptation that is Jesus' victory. And the outcome, as the chapter continues with a description of the opening of the ministry, is that Jesus is able to speak as the true messiah, not the false one of the temptations – 'his word was with authority'(v.32) – *precisely because he has refused slavery to the demonic.* Jesus' own refusal to succumb to temptation is the source of his power ('in the power of the spirit', v.14) to wage successful war against those very forces which hold human life in subjection. That must surely be why Luke shows him as victorious against attempts to destroy the truth (vv. 28-30, and compare again a Pauline definition of sin as suppression of the truth, Rom.1.18) and against the mental and physical illness that is part of human bondage (vv.33-41).

According to Luke's account, then, the divine victory over evil is achieved by means of the human ministry of Jesus, and it is a victory that continues in the final crisis of that ministry. A similar theme is to be found in Mark, although he puts even greater stress on the ministry of Jesus as the reassertion of human lordship 'over a demonic and rebellious creation' (Caird 1956 p.72). The chief conclusion of this section, therefore, is that an examination of some of the biblical material has shown that Aulén is right to speak of a victory, but that it is not merely a divine victory. The victory is at once human and divine – a divine victory only because it is a human one – and although the Synoptic Gospels do not explicitly describe the ministry of Jesus as a victory, they clearly see it as in part a conflict between the authority of God represented by Jesus and that which would deny it.[1]

II The Old Testament and the New

One important feature of the material we have reviewed introduces us to a real element of continuity between the Old and New Testaments. We saw that according to Luke the outcome of the victory over temptation was Jesus' authority in both the 'spiritual' and 'physical' worlds; in fact, as the placing of the inverted commas is meant to suggest, there is in the Bible no absolute distinction made between what can be called the cosmic and moral dimen-

---

1. Many uses of the expression 'the Kingdom of God' will have close relation to the theme of the chapter, because notions of victory and the reassertion of God's kingly authority belong together, as in Luke 11.20. It is significant that this saying is followed by the Marcan passage about the binding of the strong man by Jesus.

sions of the world. Both are the creation of God, and both are conceived to be subject to bondage. To take another example, there is in the Gospel of Mark no absolute distinction between sin and sickness (Mark 2.5-12); although, equally, simplistic accounts of their relation are also rejected in a story related by John (9.1-3). The world is one, even though it also reveals a plurality of forms of being and life. When we come to look at the Old Testament background to the New Testament language of victory, we shall find that the same holds good. There are, of course, considerable differences. Of talk of the demonic, there is relatively little: in Job, for example, Satan is still part of the household of God, not an opposing power.[2] In the book of Daniel there is, indeed, talk of the defeat of political powers oppressing Israel, and that language is likely to have made its mark on the New Testament. More germane, however, is the image of the exodus, so widespread in the Old Testament. Not only is Israel's existence as a nation held to depend on a quite literal victory over the Pharaoh's forces, but the event becomes the centre of a web of imagery by which other aspects of Israel's life are illuminated. At the same time, into the web is woven also the cosmic language of Near Eastern creation myth. The result is that the victory of God over Egypt is described in language which borrows from depictions of creation as the conquest of mythical cosmic monsters, and the language is then used of God's dominion over both history and nature. Such language is later redirected to the cross in Revelation 15. Commenting on the latter work, George Caird says something which brings out

2. Even this, however, is consistent with the point made by Aulén (above p.55) that 'The deliverance of man from the power of death and the devil is at the same time his deliverance from God's judgement.' The function of Satan in Job is to effect the judgement of God upon Job, if that judgement be understood in the wide sense of testing Job's 'mettle'.

the continuity between Old and New Testament uses of the imagery of victory. 'Israel believed that her national history was the scene where God was continuing to wage war on the powers of evil until the day of final victory. "On that day the Lord... will punish Leviathan... and will kill the dragon in the sea" (Isa. 27.1)' (Caird 1966 p.67). The Exodus was a historical event which drew to itself interpretations and expectations involving more than simply historical matters. Just as the ministry of Jesus is seen as the victory of God over the whole gamut of evils, those we call moral and those we call physical, so the Exodus came to represent not only Israel's past liberation, but also other saving events in her history and ultimately the universal future victory of God.

There is, then, in the Bible much encouragement for those who wish to see the metaphor of victory used in connection with God's saving activity. But, against Aulén, it must also be emphasised that we do not find the basis for a *theory* of the atonement, particularly if such a theory is opposed to other supposed alternatives. In the first place, we have drawn our support from only parts of the biblical talk of God's saving activity. What we find is a tradition of using a group of metaphors, in different ways but also and particularly in conjunction with images drawn from other fields of human activity than the military. For example, in speaking of the conquering lion of Judah, the author of Revelation combines the language of victory with that of sacrifice and the slave market: 'for thou wast slain and by thy blood didst ransom men for God' (Rev.5.9). Conversely, the writer to the Hebrews, whose almost sole source of metaphor is the world of priesthood and sacrifice, can yet spill over, so to speak, into other spheres and speak of Christ's sharing our humanity so 'that through death he might destroy him who has the power of death, that is, the

61

devil' (Heb.2.14). In all this we are presented with metaphors which qualify each other, helping each other to define the way in which they find their meaning. And so the Bible provides us with examples of the point made in Chapter 2 (above pp.37ff) that by metaphor we are able to understand not the whole of some reality, but parts of it, and in a way that leaves open possibilities for a further deepening of understanding. The language of victory does not then give us a *theory*, something final and fixed for ever, but one way into the many-sided reality with which we are concerned. It helps us, that is to say, to come to a measure of understanding of some aspects of the way in which the Bible sets forth in language the saving action of God in and towards his world.

So far, however, the enquiry has been largely historical, looking at some of the ways in which a metaphor was used in the books of the Bible. That is only a beginning, for there awaits us a further question. Are these only literary constructions, of interest for the way they show us how certain ancient writers thought, or do they still provide the means whereby we may now engage with the way our world really is? Can we in any way conceive of a God who wins victories by his action in and towards the world? In particular, is all that talk of demons simply a survival from primitive times? That latter question is perhaps the most difficult of all, and we shall begin with it.

III *The Language of Demons*

As the Christian tradition took shape during the early centuries, the way in which Satan and the demonic realm came to be understood underwent some changes. In particular, there was an increasing tendency to personify the devil as an individual being defeated by Christ on the cross. On the whole, as time passes, there is rather less restraint shown in the way in which the devil is depicted. As Aulén has noticed, there is a real contrast between Paul's treatment of the matter and that of later thinkers, in that 'he makes considerably less mention of the devil than most of the Fathers' (p.67). This relative lack of restraint in the later period is revealed also in a tendency to picture the defeat of the devil as a kind of deceit, in which the devil, believing that Jesus is merely a human victim, swallows him, only to be impaled on the hidden hook of his divinity. Gregory of Nyssa is clearly uncomfortable, though not uncomfortable enough, with such a conception. 'For in a way it was a fraud and deception for God, when he placed himself in the power of the enemy who was our master, not to show his naked deity, but to conceal it in our nature, and so escape recognition' (Gregory of Nyssa, *Address on Religious Instruction* 26).

A number of features of this way of putting the matter are highly questionable. In the first place, it should be noted that in the gospel accounts of the healing of those possessed by demons, the demons often recognise who it is that faces them (e.g. Mark 3.11). While too much should not be made of this, it does suggest that a theory like Gregory's is rather lacking in biblical support. Second, the dubious rationality and morality of such a conception led later thinkers, especially those in the Western tradition, to stress in contrast the moral and legal dimensions, with the very outcome that Aulén finds so problematic. We appear to be faced with a choice between a rather rationalistic and moralistic theory, and one which is both irrational and immoral. As I hope to show later, it is a false choice. But the problem with Gregory's way of putting the matter is revealed by the third feature we have to notice, and this is its tendency to be what has come to be called mythological. The battle is conceived to be fought in a sphere outside the course of concrete divine-human relations. We can contrast here two features of the gospel narratives we have noted: both the temptations and the healings are actual human encounters with evil, theologically conceived. In Gregory, on the other hand, the metaphorical dimension has fallen into the background, the victory is understood too literally, and the result is that *too much* is known about what is supposed to have happened.

The reference to the tendency of the tradition to become mythological brings us to a distinction of immense importance: that between metaphor and myth. Those who spoke too *literally* of the devil having obtained rights over mankind of which he was deprived by deceit had, in effect, failed to appreciate the metaphorical nature of the language they were using. It is as if, when Mark reports Jesus as saying that he had come to give his life as a ransom for many, we were to speculate about how much money was to be handed over and to whom (Mark 10.45). We have here an example of what some thinkers have claimed happens when a metaphor is taken too literally: it becomes a myth (see Turbayne 1970 p.60). This is not something that happens only in theology, for it can be seen to operate also in the philosophy of science. Douglas Berggren has argued that a scientific myth is what develops when an imaginative construct becomes identified with the theory it helps to create (Berggren 1963 p.458). One of the fathers of modern scientific theory, Descartes, provides an instructive example. We have already seen (above p.30) how Descartes' 'I have described the Earth and the whole visible universe *as if it were* a machine' appears to reveal an awareness of the metaphorical character of words. Unimaginative successors of Descartes have taken this and such words as *machine*, *force* and *attraction* literally, and created the myth that the world *is* a machine. We may suppose something similar to have happened to the restrained use the Bible makes of the language of the demonic, with the result that the language has fallen into greater disrepute than was necessary.

What, then, is to be made of biblical and other theological language which uses language of this kind? G.B. Caird speaks as follows about the principalities and powers in the New Testament:

> They stand, as their names imply, for the political, social, economic and religious structures of power... of the old world order which Paul believed to be obsolescent. When therefore he claims that on the cross Christ has disarmed the powers and triumphed over them, he is talking about earthly realities, about the impact of the crucifixion on the corporate life of men and nations. He is using mythical language of great antiquity and continuing vitality to interpret the historic event of the cross. (Caird 1980 p.242)

On such an account we can understand Paul to be using mythical language in a non-mythological way. If Caird is right, we have discovered another qualification of Aulén's account. The victory is not over forces which inhabit a transcendent world, separate from ours, and intervene from outside, as Aulén's account might appear to suggest. Paul is speaking about 'earthly realities... the corporate life of men and nations'. But they are not forces which can adequately be described in everyday empirical terms. The forces are 'cosmic' in the sense that they *as a matter of fact affect the way things are on earth*, not simply as aspects, but as qualifications of them. These biblical metaphors, then, are ways of describing realistically what can be described only in the indirect manner of this kind of language. But an indirect description is still a description of what is really there.

Aulén's observation that 'among the powers which hold man in bondage he (Paul) ranges the Law; and this is the most striking point of contrast between his view and that of the Fathers' (p.67) allows us to illustrate the claim that is being made. It is possible to interpret Paul's usage as implying that he believed the law to be a kind of independent suprahuman reality, a mythical entity interfering from above in human affairs. A more likely understanding, however, is that it is a metaphorical way of referring to human religious bondage. The law, according to Paul, is holy, the good gift of God to the world (Rom.7.12); but, as usurper of the place of God, it becomes the vehicle of demonic enslavement. So it is with the New Testament language of the demonic in general. The texts present us not with superhuman hypostases trotting about the world, but with *the metaphorical characterisation of moral and cosmic realities which would otherwise defy expression.*

The New Testament metaphors are not, therefore, merely literary constructions or myths, 'perspectives' of the primitive mind on the world. The writers mean us to understand the demonic realistically, but in an appropriately indirect manner. But can we share their insights? Some would claim that such ways of speaking are gone for ever, the victims of the relentless advance of scientific rationality. However, as we move from interpretation of the Bible to contemporary systematic questions, we must bear in mind the possibility that recent interpreters are justified in seeing a major difference between the New Testament and later theologians, and that the matter has become obscured by the tendency of Origen and others to conceive the powers as essentially transcendent forces. If this is so, it will be possible with the help of insights taken from the theory of metaphor to steer a middle course between a naïvely supernaturalist view of the demonic and a reductionist one, in which it is construed as a way of speaking of merely finite or psychological influences. The language of the demonic will then be seen as a way of speaking of the more than simply empirical bondage from which God incarnate in Jesus of Nazareth sets us free.

It is at this very place that a feature of some recent writing is of interest. Although outside strongly biblicist circles the devil or demons are not often mentioned, *the demonic* is an expression in fashionable use, on the lips of psychiatrists and philosophers, novelists and theologians. The latter more general and less anthropomorphic expression avoids some of the features of biblical language with which we are least comfortable, for example the descriptions of devils being thrown out of bodies like squatters from derelict property. (Even that simile, however, should not be dismissed as entirely inappropriate.) It is also more clearly conceptual and, of course, has an advantage in being ambiguous: it could refer, on the one hand, to psychological or other forces within the individual or society; or, on the other, to something more dualistic, an alien reality which enslaves the person or group believed to be so afflicted. To translate the question into the terms of the discussion of metaphor, we should ask whether biblical and other talk of the demonic is simply a metaphorical way of speaking of intra-personal realities, and so has to be translated ('demythologised') into entirely other terms; or whether it is irreducibly metaphorical, because that is the only way in which such phenomena can be appropriately characterised. In the latter case it would have to be shown that the language is worth retaining because it enables us to hold in tension both the personal and the extra-personal aspects of the condition, ascribing the possession of the person or society so affected to forces which are not simply psychological but that and more.

A recent paper by Stewart Sutherland, in which he discusses different interpretations of the characters of Raskolnikov and others in *Crime and Punishment*, enables us to develop this theme. What is the nature of the evil traits displayed by these and other of Dostoyevsky's 'demonic' characters? One interpreter, an adherent of psychoanalysis, would explain them simply in terms of a theory of human nature. Unfortunately, argues Sutherland, such a theory fails to do justice to the complexity and opaqueness of the characters. Another interpreter uses different language altogether, speaking of one who 'betrays himself to the powers of dark necessity' (Sutherland 1978 p.224). Sutherland does not himself wish to espouse or justify this 'resort... to the language of myth' (p.235), but he clearly finds it more satisfactory than those theories which hold that it is enough to speak in terms of human motives. The interpreter who speaks of 'Svidrigailov's having fallen "under the power of impersonal cosmic forces" ' is at least nearer to expressing the 'absolute rather than relative disruption' which Dostoyevsky portrays (p.233). For Sutherland, then, language of 'cosmic forces', 'the demonic', etc., while not reducible to subjective terms can be construed adequately in the language of objective good and evil.

Some modern writers, however, wish to take the metaphor of the demonic even more seriously and realistically, among them the philosopher Dorothy Emmet in her recent *The Moral Prism*. There she gives some detailed attention to the nature of what she calls the daemonic person. Alluding like Stewart Sutherland to Dostoyevsky, she speaks of not just a 'moral badness, but a corruption of the springs of action in a person's mind' (Emmet 1979 p.151).[3] 'Those, both Greek and German, who have written about the daemonic have been drawn to talk of it not just in

---

3. It is significant that Rollo May (1970 pp.130f) attributes the failure of Western liberals to recognise the demonic character of Hitler's regime to their blindness to this kind of reality.

psychological and sociological terms, but in mythological and metaphysical ones, where a drive coming from the deep self acquires cosmic overtones' (p.78).

Professor Emmet does not elaborate these 'cosmic overtones', but some account of them must be attempted if we are to come to a satisfactory understanding of the world of metaphor with which we are concerned. If we are neither to give a purely psychological account, with the attendant danger of failing to do justice to the objective reality of evil; nor to understand the demonic of the Bible in such tendentious terms that it appears ridiculously primitive; then we must come to terms with the fact that in this area of discourse we meet an attempt to express the objectivity and irrationality of evil in the only way in which it can adequately be expressed: as a reality generating its own momentum and sweeping up human beings into its power. Human life is lived in interrelationship with other human beings and with the world, leaving on one side for a moment the so-called 'vertical' relationship with God. We are what we are partly by virtue of that network of relationships. When it goes badly awry, the person or society is rightly described as enslaved, another familiar metaphor in this connection.

We are speaking, then, of extreme cases of moral enslavement, alienation or depravity which are not adequately characterised by subjective, psychological or moral language alone. The demonic person is so bound up with the universe that there results a slavery which is metaphysical and not simply moral. That is why the great exponents of Christian atonement theology have never been content to see the person independently of the environment, so that both sin and salvation have been conceived to embrace both the moral and the cosmic dimensions of life. Aulén's book here calls attention to a strength of the Eastern tradition, which, with its tendency to moralise, the West has tended to neglect. This is a feature of our topic to which we shall have repeatedly to return. Here what must be stressed is that the 'classic' theory, with its insistence on calling attention to the context in which our life is lived, has much to teach us about both sin and salvation.

The language of possession by demonic forces, then, is used to express the helplessness of human agents in the face of psychological, social and cosmic forces in various combinations. Theologically, we must see the origins of the bondage in the idolatrous worship of that which is not God. When we give any part of the created world the value of God, we thus far come into the power of a reality which, because it is not divine, operates demonically. 'The demonic,' wrote Tillich, 'is the elevation of something conditional to unconditional significance' (Tillich 1968 vol.I p.155); it is the 'claim of something finite to infinity or to divine greatness' (vol. III p.109). As an illustration, we might take Kierkegaard's account of the demonic in *Either/ Or*: 'Don Juan... is the expression for the daemonic determined as the sensuous; Faust, its expression determined as the intellectual or spiritual' (Kierkegaard 1843/1959 vol.I p.89). It might therefore be argued that any element of our relationship with our fellow human beings and the world can *become* demonised. Accordingly, the psychiatrist Rollo May defines what he calls the daimonic as 'any natural function which has the power to take over the whole person', giving as examples 'sex and eros, anger and rage, and the craving for power' (May 1970 p.123). For those who find this too narrowly psychological, there is the saying of Aristotle which so fascinated E.R. Dodds and Freud before him: 'For nature is daemonic' (Dodds 1951 p.120).

Here we come to an important and illuminating difference between the view some Greek thinkers would hold of the demonic and that which seems the tendency of the biblical writings. To say that nature is demonic is for much of Hellenism tantamount to saying that it is divine. Like nature, the human soul also has inherent within it the seeds of divinity. Dodds believes this doctrine to derive from the myth of the Titans' eating of the infant god Dionysus and the springing of humanity from what remained when Zeus destroyed them with his thunderbolt (p.155). Whatever the origin, the doctrine made the Greeks ambivalent about the material world: it could be seen either as in some way divine or as evil. A good example is Plato's rather ambiguous attitude to the 'madness' of artistic inspiration. In the *Phaedrus* alone does he allow it any positive value (*Phaedrus* 244); elsewhere he rejects it in favour of a strict rationalism. Plato's attitude to inspiration serves to reveal the heart of the Greek understanding of the demonic: it indicated the ecstatic, the irrational, the intuitive, that which welled up, so to speak, from the inner god for both good and ill. It was morally ambiguous, and so for Plato nearly always suspect.

The tendency of biblical thought is otherwise. Two features indicate the contrast with the Hellenic: the fact that both nature and human life, as the creation of God, are good, and in no way morally ambiguous; and the fact that the Hebrews maintain a stricter distinction between God and everything else, whether 'natural' or demonic. The demonic is not therefore conceived as the divine in some way immanent in the world, but something that happens to the world to throw it out of kilter. In the beginning, nothing is demonic in itself, not even Satan (see, again, Job 1). The demonic is what happens when what is in itself good is corrupted into its opposite. A biblical writer would, then, be unlikely to say that nature is demonic, but he might agree that it *becomes* demonic in certain of its relationships with the human creation. Any part of the created world, accordingly, can become the vehicle of demonic disruption. Examples of how sex or the intellect can become demonised have already been cited. If the created order, or a part of it, is treated as god, then it behaves like god for those who so treat it, but for destructive rather than creative ends. The feature of modern life that we find it easiest to understand in these terms is power, as it is seen to operate in different dimensions of our life: psychological, social, economic, political and cosmic. Part of the wide appeal of Tolkien's *Lord of the Rings* appears to derive in part from the fact that a constant theme is that to use power in certain ways is to be possessed by it. Similarly, more psychologically subtle depictions of the demonisation of power are to be seen in characters like Dostoyevsky's Stavrogin. A more abstract point is that Western civilisation as a whole appears to be in danger of being possessed by power, whether we consider the effects of our domination by machinery ('technocracy') or by military developments which appear to be impossible to control.

All these cases, and particularly the demonisation of power, are illuminated for us by a passage from scripture we have already met: 'If you, then, will worship me, it shall all be yours' (Luke 4.7). The implication of the story of Jesus' temptation is that to use power idolatrously is to be possessed by it, as by a demon. Similarly, the New Testament's attitude to political authorities shows that the political order is created good, but can become demonised. There is accordingly no contradiction between the recommendations of submission to political authority in Romans 13 and the rejection of that authority underlying what is said in Revelation 13. In the latter passage, the relationship between the state and the Christian had been thrown out of order because 'men worshipped the dragon, for he had given his authority to the beast, and they worshipped the beast' (Rev.13.4). One of the keys to an understanding of the message of that passage is the repeated 'worshipped': divine honours were paid to that which was merely created. As one commentator on the passage says, 'All political power is the gift of God; but when men deify the state, either directly by a religious cult or indirectly by demanding for it the total loyalty and obedience that are due to God alone, it ceases to be human and becomes bestial' (Caird 1966 p.162). What was created good becomes demonic.

The language of the demonic, then, is language which enables us to bring to expression the fact of the subjection of human moral agents to forces they are unable to control. It should also be apparent that talk of moral agents should not be understood merely individualistically. There have been times in history when it appears that whole societies have been in a kind of moral slavery, as is often said to have been the case with Hitler's Germany. Here it must be noticed that the social slavery was not absolute, in that certain prophetic figures were able to break through the moral blindness, though not in such a way as to make a significant impact. The point is that human beings do in different ways appear to fall into the grip of alien forces, which leave them not only incapable of acting morally but also of distinguishing between good and evil. It is, according to Professor Emmet, a characteristic of the demonic person that he or she claims to be beyond good and evil, superior to the moral distinctions that trouble ordinary people (Emmet 1979 ch.7). Here we find another important link with biblical conceptions. Idolatry, giving divine status to that which is not God, is the ultimate falsehood, the submission to the lie. From it flows the inability to speak and do the truth in other spheres, too; and so there results a slavery which has implications for other aspects of human life, intellectual, moral and indeed physiological.[4]

The examples which have been used to show what demonic possession means are for the most part extreme cases. They enable us to see the nature of the slavery writ large, so to speak. In the great literary depictions, the very difference of the characters from the ordinary enables us to see the horror of demonic moral behaviour. But the characters are great also because they cast light on the plight of the rest of us, at least as we are apart from grace. In other words, the metaphors with which we have been concerned in this section become one of the means by which we come to be aware of the human condition, providing as they do the sombre backcloth against which the doctrine of the atonement has always been expressed and understood. And it is that human condition which, according to Aulén, was healed and freed from its self-inflicted enemies on the cross, conceived as a great divine victory.

IV   The Language of Victory

So much, then, for the language of the demonic: it *can* mean something; or rather, it is an essential way of speaking if we are to understand certain features of our fallen world. Can the same be done for the language of victory? We begin with what Aulén sees to be one of the chief advantages of this way of speaking of the atonement: rather than loading all of the weight on the cross, it conceives the victory as being the outcome of the incarnation, life, death and resurrection taken as a narrative whole. (That is, of course, not the way that Aulén speaks, but it helps to make the point that we do not centre our understanding of the meaning of Jesus on one part only of his story.) The New Testament supports such a

4. May it not be that the much discussed sin against the Holy Spirit (Matt12.31f) is to be understood in terms of a blindness that is such that even the Spirit of Truth is rejected as its opposite – the final slavery to the lie?

view, as we have seen, either using the language of victory or recording events that can be so interpreted in connection with all aspects of the story: the incarnation; the temptation, and obedience of Jesus to his Father in general; the cross and resurrection. The cross represents the completion of the pattern already made manifest in the life; the resurrection the completion and revelation of the cross as being of universal significance. Where this account differs from that of Aulén is in seeing the victory as more than the miraculous transformation of human possibilities effected by the death on the cross. There is indeed a miraculous transformation of possibilities, but only in so far as a liberation from bondage is signalled, created and promised by means of a human victory over evil.

The human significance of the victory can be understood if we isolate the primary field on which it is fought: the entry of Jesus upon one course of action rather than another. The fact that he did one kind of thing rather than another is an indication of what kind of life pattern he followed, and therefore of the place where the character of the victory is to be sought. Once again, the temptation narratives are of crucial importance, for they depict the choice of one approach to the exercise of power rather than another. The first place where we shall therefore find the meaning of the metaphor of victory is the refusal of Jesus to exercise power demonically. We can call this, using a metaphor which has perhaps sprung from it, a moral victory, though it is also more than that. We can also understand it as in some way belonging to the 'inner' rather than the outer life of Jesus. By this is meant not that we can discover certain facts about the consciousness of Jesus, but that, as the stories of temptation and trial are told, we can *see* the conquest of the demonic happening through the decision for obedience.

But it is not simply a matter of human import. We have already seen something of how the theological significance of this choice is set out in such passages as Luke 4. For Luke, the authority of Jesus' ministry derives from the choice of one pattern of life rather than another. That is the reason why the Synoptic Gospels see the ministry of Jesus at another level than the human, as God's activity in overcoming the alienation of mankind from both moral and cosmic aspects of our situation. The healings and exorcisms are part of a process in which human life is seen *and made* whole: 'release to the captives, and recovering of sight to the blind' belong together. Both are part of liberation from human bondage, both aspects of the event in which God sets us free by means of the activity of his Son. Just as bondage to the demonic is both moral and physical, so is release. If, then, the victory is, at different levels, both human and divine, we can, as Aulén wishes, understand the cross in continuity with the ministry, as its natural outcome. Yet with the main lines of the Western tradition we can also understand that it is the heart of the matter, the place where the battle against evil comes to a climax. That the evangelists give different emphases to their interpretations of the death of Jesus is not a problem here. What they, along with other New Testament writers, have in common, is that they understand it as the appropriate outcome of Jesus's life, the so to speak logical consequence of the person he was and the choices he made. There is a human moral victory which is construed in different ways as the freeing of human life from bondage precisely because it is also the victory of God over disorderly moral, political and cosmic forces.

How, then, should we understand this encounter between Jesus and the demonic? It is an encounter – *the* encounter – between the power of God undemonically exercised by a man and moral, social and political forces demonically exercised by others. That means that we should be careful not to understand the cross as a suffering of a purely passive kind. It is, without doubt, passive in one way: that Jesus is seen to submit to rather than resist violently those who represent the powers of evil that wish to see him out of the way. The absolute sureness with which the Fourth Gospel represents Jesus as going to his death is sometimes held to be 'docetic', as if it is no longer a truly human action. Equal sense, however, is made of it if we see it as John's way of showing that the passion is active also. It is an exercise of authority which, because it does not *succumb to* the typical human temptation to violence, is a submission which consists in a refusal to submit. Some early Christian preaching, as represented in the speeches recorded in Acts, appears to have seen the cross as a defeat which the resurrection turned to victory. In one sense, it was that. But in another, as later reflection appears to have concluded, it is more profound to see it as the heart of the victory. That is why Paul shares the insight of the Fourth Gospel when he holds the death of Jesus to be an exercise of divine power (1 Cor. 1f), while, as we have seen, the author of Revelation interprets the triumph of the Lion of Judah through the imagery of a slaughtered lamb.

To describe the cross as a victory is to use a metaphor in a bold way. It is what Ricoeur calls a 'category mistake that clears the way to a new vision' (Ricoeur 1977 p.230). It means that the cross is metaphorically but really a victory, and a victory whose significance is to be expressed in several ways. First, it 'clears the way to a new vision' because it is revelatory of the nature of human life on earth. To be victorious does not mean butchering your opponent with weapons, but refusing to exercise power demonically in order to overcome evil with good. (That is the point of Rom.12.14-21, whose climax is a clear reference to the atoning cross: 'Do not be overcome by evil, but overcome evil with good', v.21). An enemy is indeed in such a way deprived of power – so that there is a real victory – but at the same time the real enemy is revealed to be not the opposing human being but the forces which hold all human life in thrall. The notion that the metaphor is in some way revelatory is very important here. Part of the meaning of the demonic is, as we saw, that it makes us slaves to the lie, to the inability to tell truth from falsity, good from evil. To understand Jesus' death as a victory is to be set free from false conceptions of life (see here Caird 1956 pp.84ff). Jesus submits to the power of the lie in order to reveal it as such and so to lay open the possibility for the truth. It was therefore a sure instinct and not merely a drive to be systematic that led Barth to expand the slogan 'Jesus is the Victor' in terms of his witnessing to the truth (Barth 1959/1961 pp.165ff). The lie in this context refers to the behaviour of anything finite or created – and that includes political and ecclesiastical institutions – which is treated as or elevates itself to be of divine status. Idolatry in all its forms is revealed to be demonic, the opponent of the conquering Christ, by Jesus' refusal, at the cost of his own death, of the allurements of any other means of success than the genuinely human.

This use of metaphor is revelatory of human life in another sense, too. It is one of the features of a successful use of metaphor that it not only illuminates that of which it speaks – the ministry and death of Jesus and the ethics of those who base their lives on it – but by a kind of reverse movement also that area of discourse and behaviour from which its main meaning used to be drawn. Thus we may think that the word *victory* applies literally and primarily to a process of military action, but the transformation of meaning in which we are involved will teach us that we are wrong. A real victory is the kind of thing that happens when Jesus goes to the cross. In this a metaphor may enable us to change our way of thinking, *and therefore our world*. Towards the end of Chapter 2 it was argued that there are cases where the theological use of a term, far from being parasitic on some supposed 'ordinary' meaning, is rather the standard by which other uses may be judged. Here is an excellent example of such a transformation of meaning by a theological term. And it follows that those who tread the way of the cross are committed to a kind of living in the world that reproduces this form of victory under the conditions in which we live.

Second, to understand the history of Jesus as a victory clears the way for a new vision of *the world*. The exorcisms and healings are, as we have seen, the re-ordering of life on earth to the end for which it was created. That is why St John the Divine shows us that the final end of the victory of the slaughtered lamb is a new heaven and a new earth (Rev. 21). The point of his vision is not, however, some mythological future, for it is centred in the reality which is the incarnation. The incarnation, the presence of God the Word in and to the created world, shows us both the goodness and fallenness of the world in which we live: subject to bondage, but awaiting the final revelation of the children of God (Rom.8.19). This teaches us something that has often been neglected in the West, with its tendency to limit its understanding of the atonement to the moral or juridical. The process of redemption, begun in the incarnation, continued and promised in the Spirit, is not concerned simply with the reformation of the moral person, but with the recapitulation of all things in Christ: the extension of the benefits of the divine victory to all parts of the created order. However we are to understand the implications of such claims as those of Col.1.20 ('through him – Christ – to reconcile to himself all things') and Eph.1.10 ('to unite all things in him'), this much surely is clear, that the Christian understanding of salvation, when seen with the assistance of this metaphor, is of the redemption of mankind not out of or without but along with the world in which we are set. The American politician who is reported to have said that environmental pollution is of no matter because of the imminent return of Christ had missed this central dimension of soteriology. The victory of Christ is in part the re-establishment of the rule of God over a demonised creation, so that it too may reveal and praise its creator.

The third and perhaps for our purposes the central point about the clearing of the way to new vision is that the metaphor of victory enables us to bring God to speech. We do not, in telling the story of Jesus, merely narrate a series of tales which may or may not illuminate contemporary life on earth. If the victory of Jesus is the victory of God, then the language in which the story is told is one of the ways in which we are enabled to speak of God. We learn, that is, that God is the kind of being who makes his presence felt in our world in the way in which the life and death of Jesus take shape. The metaphor of victory is therefore one of the means by which God is enabled to come to human speech as a *saving* God. We are given a real but limited knowledge of the action and therefore of the being of God through the way in which Jesus does the conquering work of the Father.

There are, to be sure, limits to what can be claimed for this knowledge. The teaching that the life and death of Jesus, even understood in the light of his resurrection, are a victory over the dark forces which afflict our world, is problematic in other ways than those presented by modern rationalism. It does not appear to be a victory, because demonic evil still appears to be in control of things. If the cross of Jesus is so decisive in determining the direction of the world, why is this not so more palpably? We meet here the problem that has so troubled modern Christianity, of the relevance of past history to present reality. Such answer as can be given to this question requires a chapter to itself. But the point has been introduced here because it bears on the question at the heart of this chapter, the *meaning* of the metaphorical description of the cross as victory. It has already been claimed that the meaning is to be found in the revelatory quality of the language, especially as it enables us to bring God to human language, but more generally as it opens our eyes to the nature of the human plight and its healing. But if there is revelation, it must also be remembered that in this area particularly the meaning of our language can only be understood eschatologically, which means in terms of that which shall be. The cross can be understood only as promise and as it is contradicted in the denial of its truth by a fallen creation. The tension of the 'now but not yet' is expressed by many of the biblical expressions we have already met: that Satan has been cast out of heaven, presumably to operate on earth, where he 'prowls around like a roaring lion, seeking someone to devour' (1 Pet.5.8); that 'the God of hope will soon crush Satan under your feet' (Rom.16.20). But perhaps the clearest treatment of the eschatological character of the victory is to be found in 1 Cor.15. The risen Christ, says Paul, 'must reign until he has put all his enemies under his feet'(v.25). Yet he justifies the *promise* by an appeal to a victory that has taken place. 'For God has put all things in subjection under his feet' (v.27, citing the anthropological text Ps.8.6, which is used in a similar way in Heb.2.6ff). The past victory is guarantee of a future consummation ('when all things are subjected to him' v.28) and the locus of a present struggle.

The metaphor, that is to say, operates in the space be-tween what has happened and what is promised.

Accordingly, the reason why we must speak of these things in metaphor is not that we are ignorant of divine realities, and can speak only of our experience. Metaphor is the appropriate way to speak in the present of God's action in and towards his world. There is a victory, won, being won and to be won. It is God's victory, for it completes, in face of those forces which would disrupt it, the purposes of the good creation. But its realisation, and its expression in language, come to be only through the presence to the world of God's free Spirit, God enabling the world to become that which it is intended to be. Metaphor, then, – when it, too, is filled with meaning by gift of that same Spirit – expresses the truth of this matter, which is God present savingly to his world, but in ways appropriate to the nature of the world in its createdness and fallenness; that is, in the victory that is the life of Jesus Christ. We shall find that other metaphors operate in distinctive but similar ways.

4

The Justice of God: A Conversation

Like doth quit like, and Measure still for
Measure.
Shakespeare, Measure for Measure, V.i.407

I Overlaps

As we move from one family of metaphors to another, we
must be aware that they do not operate in self-contained
worlds. Indeed, the great advantage of an approach to the
nature of language by a study of metaphor is that it makes it
possible to conceive something of the openness of concepts
to each other, and so to allow for nuances and shades of
meaning to be developed. In this chapter we shall concentrate attention on the use in the theology of atonement of
language deriving from the world of law. In one way,
something quite different will be found to emerge, for the
reason that the language is different, and it therefore enables
distinct aspects of the relation between God and the world
to come into view. But it is not something completely
different, as reference to a biblical passage referred to in the
previous chapter will reveal.

Satan began his biblical career, certainly as he appears in
the prologue of the book of Job, as a member of God's
household. He was the 'left hand' of God, the adversary or
counsel for the prosecution, testing Job to see of what mettle he was made: whether he really did serve God for naught.
He had therefore a legal function, representing the rule of
law, order and punishment. His defeat, therefore – whatever
the significance of his fall to earth in Luke and Revelation –

signifies that the will of God is not to be identified with abstract legal justice (Caird 1956 p.37). God is revealed by the cross as one who bears the power of the demonic rather than punishes those who have fallen into its power.

The contribution made by a theology of the demonic, and the consequent taking seriously of the place of Satan in the New Testament, is that it presents a picture of evil as an appalling and irrational corruption of the good creation, something that cannot be explained away because it is a denial of the purposes of God. The cross of Jesus does not serve to explain such evil, but to act: to break its power by undergoing its concentrated opposition. The advantages of such apparently mythological ways of speaking in this context are that they enable us to speak about the nature of evil and its continuing power, and point to its symptoms and outcome in the idolatrous misuse and worship of that which is not God. However, the vices of such a way of speaking follow from its virtues: the danger is that by stressing the irrational and uncontrollable it may minimize the part played by responsible human agents in the process. That has not been entirely ignored in the account that has been given of idolatry and the submission to the lie: it is only after the choice of evil has been made that slavery results. As Coleridge wrote, 'A will cannot be *free* to choose evil – for in the very act it forfeits its freedom, and so becomes a corrupt Nature, self-enslaved' (cited, J.R. Barth, 1969, p.110). But if we are to understand in what respect human beings are slaves, a clearer account is required of the nature of their slavery and our reponsibility for it. It is here that legal imagery has its part to play in the theology of both sin and salvation. Sin is often conceived as transgression of the law of God, and, correlatively, salvation is understood as freedom from the consequences or penalties of that transgression.

Even this, however, is not as simple as it may on the surface appear. There are a number of complicating factors, biblical, historical and systematic. The first is that in both Old and New Testaments there is no interest in law abstractly and as such. In the law books of the Old Testament, for example, there is a certain amount of variety in the way the law is conceived to function in Israel's life, but none about the fact that it belongs firmly in the context of God's covenant with Israel. The laws and instructions are a gift of God, the framework for the communal life of those whom God set free from Egypt. Similarly, the punishments and penalties are concerned both to uphold the integrity of the community's life and to restore the relationship with God which that transgression disrupts. Furthermore, the laws are also in close relationship with the cult for which they give directions. The result is that the metaphors of law and sacrifice come to be very closely intertwined in the tradition. In the New Testament, when they are both used to speak of the death of Jesus, they interpret each other, perhaps classically in Rom.3.24f, where Paul combines them with a third image, the slave market: 'they are justified... through the redemption which is in Christ Jesus, whom God put forward as an expiation'.

The second complicating factor is the way in which the legal aspects of the atonement were developed in Christian theology in the West. It is sometimes remarked that many of the early Latin Fathers were lawyers who were predisposed to express the relations of God and humankind in legal terms. It is to this tradition that we owe the introduction of the concept of satisfaction into the theology of the atonement. This, at any rate, was Harnack's view, and there seems little reason to contradict him:

> Here, as in almost all departments of activity in the Latin Church, it was of the highest moment that

> Tertullian, the jurist, and Cyprian, the ecclesiastical ruler, were the first Latin theologians. Disinclined for philosophical and strictly religious speculation, and dominated by a prosaic but powerful moralism, the Latins were possessed from the first of an impulse to carry religion into the legal sphere. (Harnack 1885/ 1897 p.310)

Harnack sees the development as deriving from relatively minor beginnings: 'Tertullian used the expression *"satisfacere deo"* about men... but, so far as I know, not about the work of Christ' (Harnack 1885/1896 p.294). That is to say, the human relationship to God was spoken of in terms of our 'satisfying' God's requirements, but it was not yet said that Christ in some way satisfied them in our stead or on our behalf. The use of the word *satisfaction* to describe what was achieved on the cross was the achievement of Cyprian, and is described by Harnack in a manner which is highly unsympathetic but which also indicates why this approach to the theology of the atonement has fallen into disrepute:

> But Cyprian also applied the *"satisfacere deo"* to Christ himself... His suffering and death constituted a sacrifice presented by Christ to God in order to propitiate him... The angry God whom it was necessary to propitiate and of whom the Greeks knew so little, became more and more familiar in the West. (Harnack 1885/1897 p.312)

Whether it was so stark a matter is open to dispute. What is right is that there developed in the West a tendency to conceive the human relation to God largely in terms of legal obligations (and, it might be added, a corresponding perplexity in the Eastern churches about Western atonement theology as a whole). The central motif is demand: the human agent is expected to fulfil certain obligations. In default of them, there must be either a penalty or some other means of compensation. There are parallels between this and the Old Testament dispensation, where certain obligations are set before Israel, obligations whose breach were condemned by the prophets in no uncertain terms. But in the latter, the framework is different, deriving as it does from the personal relation of gracious God and covenant people. Without doubt, many Western theologies of atonement have tended to be legalistic, making it appear that God is a God of law before he is a God of love, rather than the reverse, and so failing to do justice to the personal, relational, aspects of the matter. But that is not true of the Western tradition at its best, as we shall discover in the next section.

II Anselm of Canterbury

It was Anselm of Canterbury who achieved the definitive systematic treatment of the atonement in terms of *satisfaction*. Because his account is now widely rejected every care must be taken to understand what he has to say (see especially McIntyre 1954, von Balthasar 1984). It is important to remember also that Anselm's is one of the first essays in a systematic theology of the atonement, attempting to bring intellectual shape to an area where there had been much disorder. Anselm was sharply critical of what had been until his time the chief accounts of the matter. As the histories of doctrine show, a number of theologies of the atonement existed side by side in the centuries before him, and they tended to represent variations, and not always very subtle ones, on the theme of ransom. The devil, it was held, had obtained, as a result of the Fall, certain rights over humankind, either on his own account or by divine permission. Freedom from this bondage was won by means of the payment represented by the blood of Christ.

In face of a tendency to mythologise the metaphor of ransom, Anselm's achievement is immense. He wished to give a rational account of the matter, and wrote what he did because he believed that both in himself and in his ways toward us God is rational. That being so, it must be possible for the theologian to seek to gain, in the light of the divine rationality, a measure of understanding of the mysteries of the faith. There are without doubt dangers in such an approach, and it sometimes seems as if Anselm is over-systematic in his exposition of the meaning of the incarnation and atonement. But in so far as God's involvement in the reconciliation of human life to himself can be understood as a reordering of that which had become disordered – and there are strict limits to that[1] – it is not only right but necessary to seek to express in human language the inherent rationality of the process.

The theology which Anselm rejected failed the test of rationality in a number of ways. In the first place, it made the mistake of taking too literally the allusion to ransom in Mark 10.45 ('to give his life as a ransom for many'), treating the blood as an actual price and asking whether it was paid to God or to the devil. That is to go beyond anything licensed by the language of the New Testament, and produces a 'myth' of the kind we have met before (above, p.64), the result of taking a metaphor literally. Secondly, as Anselm saw, the theory of ransom was too dualistic, giving the devil too much of an autonomous authority: 'the devil and man belong to God alone, and neither one stands outside God's power; what case, then, did God have to plead with his own creature, concerning his own creature, in his own affair...?' (*Cur Deus Homo* I,vii). Anselm's argument is that even if it is right to suppose that the devil in some way inflicts

---

1. We must here take the 'in so far' with full seriousness. Our ultimate concern in this topic is not with order but with freedom: the conquest of disorder is with a view to the final freeing of the creature for the praise of God.

punishment – and we have seen something of the rationale of this imagery – he does what he does only by divine permission, and does not have to be treated with as an independent and autonomous agent. There would be nothing inherently unjust in a rescue of the enslaved without the performance required on the popular account. It follows that if the necessity of the atonement is to be demonstrated, some other account must be given.

The theology of satisfaction is an attempt to give a more adequate account of the atonement with the assistance of a metaphor drawn from the world of law. In Anselm's own words, his is a programme to show 'by necessary reasons (Christ being put out of sight, as if nothing had ever been known of him) that it is impossible for any man to be saved without him' (Preface). The theological vocabulary on which he draws is that which we have already seen emerging in Tertullian and Cyprian. God is the one to whom certain obligations are due: 'to sin is the same thing as not to render his due to God' (I,xi). It is sometimes dismissively observed that Anselm takes his view of legality from the mediaeval feudal order, and the suggestion is that this is to liken the deity to an arbitrary or oppressive ruler. The fact is, however, that the opposite is the case, and Anselm will not be understood unless this is appreciated. It was the duty of the feudal ruler to maintain the order of rights and obligations without which society would collapse. Anselm's God is understood to operate *analogously* for the universe as a whole: as the upholder of universal justice.

Anselm's argument depends upon a particular conception of justice. He holds that God cannot simply overlook breaches of the universal law. If injustice goes unpunished, the universe is shown to be an unjust and so irrational place, and the God responsible for its order no longer worthy of the name God. 'For it does not follow that if God wills to lie, it is just to lie, but rather, that he is not God.' Therefore, 'if sin is... remitted unpunished, he who sins and he who does not sin will be in the same position with God' (I,xii). The point is that God does not demand satisfaction for sin because he is in some way personally affronted or offended by transgression. What is at stake is 'the order and beauty of the universe', for which God is responsible (I,xv).

Alongside the conception of God as the upholder of universal justice is a corresponding account of the seriousness of sin. To do anything contrary to the divine will is very serious (I,xxi); therefore, for sinners to put themselves right with God is beyond their powers. Yet justice demands the satisfaction of the divine demands. 'Thus man is inexcusable, because he willingly incurred that debt, which he cannot pay, and by his own fault involved himself in this inability, so that he can pay neither what he owed before sin... nor what he owes on account of sin' (I,xxiv). It is a gloomy picture. God expects the execution of his proper demands. The framework of universal obligations has been broken, and God is, so to speak, faced with a dilemma. Either he must punish the sin, or there must be satisfaction from some other source. Here, again, we must listen very carefully if we are not to fall into the popular habit of misinterpretation. To understand the meaning of *satisfaction* in Anselm, we must take note of John McIntyre's insistence (1954 pp.86ff) that there are two concepts, *poena* and *satisfactio*, and that, in a way that may not have been true for earlier thought, they are not only different but *alternatives*. Satisfaction is therefore according to Anselm the way by which God is enabled *not* to exact a tribute of compensating penalty from the sinner. He is therefore not propounding a version of what came to be called penal substitution, in which Jesus is conceived to be punished by God in place of the sinner. There is a substitution, an exchange, but it is not primarily penal in character. McIntyre again: it is 'not in the setting of Roman law or Teutonic Wergild that the notion of satisfaction finds its proper place' (p.89).

Von Balthasar makes a similar point when he says that:

> Anselm's doctrine of redemption, his so-called doctrine of satisfaction, will have about it nothing of the "juristic". On the contrary, he is at pains to defend himself against any idea of a God of justice, "who would so delight in or stand in need of the blood of the innocent that apart from his death he would not pardon the guilty"... It is not a matter of reckoning, but of inner, ontological union. (Von Balthasar 1969/1984 p.249, citing Anselm I, x and xix)

That is not entirely accurate. There *is* something of the 'juristic' in so far as Anselm is drawing upon a legal metaphor in such a way that some connotations of the original meaning are carried over. Von Balthasar is right, however, in suggesting that the real concern is with the relation between creator and creature, not considerations of abstract justice.

What, then, is *satisfaction*? In large measure it has to do with the divine action in setting right that which has been thrown out of kilter by human sin. Anselm's belief is that unless there is some objective righting of the balance, there can be no restoration of human life even to the state it enjoyed before sin interposed. With Athanasius before him (*De Inc.* 6), he teaches that 'unless God is going to complete what he began with human nature, he made so sublime a nature for so great a good all to no purpose' (II,iv). The framework of the theology of satisfaction is thus only secondarily human fallenness; the primary focus is the goodness of God and the excellence of creation's crown. *Satisfaction* is therefore Anselm's way of speaking of that which took place as a result of the good God's being unwilling to allow his creatures to destroy themselves. It is the act of the triune God in the unity of his personal being. 'Therefore, since he himself (Jesus Christ) is God, the Son of God, he offered himself for his own honour to himself, as he did to the Father and the Holy Spirit' (II,xviii).

Such trinitarian language shows that Anselm teaches that satisfaction is something that the Son, on behalf of human-kind but also as God, offers to the Father. It is not a legal transaction, but an act of unmerited grace. There is, to be sure, a quantitative, almost transactional component to the gift: something that the incarnate Son offers to the Father to compensate for what his human creation has itself failed to offer. The death of this man, when given freely as a gift to the Father, outweighs in value all the sins of men, great and numerous as they are (II,iv). The life of the Son of God is of such value, indeed, that its effect reaches even to those who lived in another place and at another time (II,xvi). Because it is the life of the divine Son of God it is of infinite weight, enough to more than outweigh the enormous weight of sin that has accumulated (I,xxi). It is true, also, that Anselm does not stress as strongly as he might the overflowing love and grace of God, the concept of mercy being more prominent than that of love. But the development must also be seen to be true in large measure to Paul's celebration of the grace abounding, in for example Rom.5.15-21: 'where sin increased, grace abounded all the more'.

It is in this context important to note the ways in which Anselm is not bound to a literal reading of the language of cosmic legality. God is not primarily a judge who exacts a compensating penalty from Jesus as a man. Jesus as the God–man freely offers his life to the Father. Furthermore, when he is thinking in terms of the human obedience of Jesus, Anselm takes some considerable trouble to demonstrate that it is an obedience which is freely given. 'For this is simple and true obedience, when the rational nature, not of necessity but willingly, keeps the will that it has received from God' (I,x; cf II,x where Anselm makes a similar point of speaking of the matter in the light of the personal union of the divine and human in Jesus). It is also to be noted that Anselm does not put all of his eggs in the basket of satisfaction. He is also able to draw on other strands of the tradition, albeit very briefly, as when he echoes the language of the 'classic theory' by alluding to the overcoming of the devil (II,xi). Nevertheless, the main metaphor does dominate to the exclusion of almost everything else.

III Beyond the Legal Metaphor

The weaknesses of Anselm's theology of atonement have been well rehearsed in the secondary literature, perhaps most sympathetically by McIntyre (pp.186ff). Chief among them are undoubtedly the fact that too much weight is thrown on the action of Jesus Christ towards the Father, too little on the notion of salvation being realised through the involvement of the triune God in human history. Anselm rightly makes much of the humanity of the God–man, arguing that only on its basis can the human condition be healed from within (II,vi). Yet the whole affair does sometimes appear to be an exercise of power rather than love: 'the Son, with the Father and the Holy Spirit, had determined to show the loftiness of his omnipotence by no other means than death' (I,ix). Added to this is the fact that aesthetic considerations make it appear almost that God is as much concerned to achieve a correct balance of numbers in heaven as to realise his love towards the creation. (See, for example, the title of I,xvi: 'The reason why the number of the angels who fell is to be made up from among men.') More important is the often noted weakness that Anselm appears to equate salvation with the remission of penalty. Whether that is the whole story, it is true that relatively little emphasis is given to the atonement as the place where reconciliation in the sense of a renewed personal walking with God is made real. We see here a genuine difficulty, of the kind we met in Chapter 1 above, that has been felt with Western accounts of the atonement: that the cross is understood in a way that seems rather external to us, a transaction taking place in a different space and time from ours.

Once those points have been made, however, we come to realise that for all the problems of its detailed working out, the theology of Anselm introduces considerations of central importance for the theme of this book. We can understand what they are by noting that the criticisms which have just been outlined are ones which accept the main thrust of what Anselm is doing. They are criticisms which share his commitment to orthodox Christian belief. As the survey in Chapter 1 of the theology of the three representatives of modern critical thought revealed, however, there are other more damaging questions to be asked. Chief among them is this: How far is the theology of satisfaction viable in a world which has so different a conception of human freedom?[2] For our purposes, that very broad question becomes the one of whether it is possible or right to think of God as a kind of cosmic overlord. In what sense may or must we conceive God as the one responsible for universal justice? It is a real question for all eras; in one which has come to stress so strongly as ours the autonomy of the individual, it is pressing. The value of Anselm in this respect is that he enables us to understand what is at stake. He also enables us

2. 'Anselms's most important dogmatic treatises revolve around the problem of freedom... *Cur Deus Homo* demythologizes the doctrine of redemption and grounds everything in the unforced freedom of the death of the redeemer and the consequent liberation of the con-strained freedom of men' (Von Balthasar 1969/1984 p.237).

to engage from a slightly different standpoint with the questions that arose in the discussion of the atonement as victory.

In that latter discussion it was argued that one of the contributions made by an examination of the metaphor was a realisation that human life is rooted in its physical context. There can be no merely moralistic or personalistic discussion of salvation which does not root human life in the context of the created order as a whole. Human alienation derives in part from wrong relations with the world about us, where the creation is idolatrously misused and sweeps up human agents into its power. By contrast with that, the theology of satisfaction tends to concentrate on the legal and moral rather than the cosmic aspects of the divine–human relationship. In that respect, it is a characteristically Western development, and is bounded on one side by Augustine's preoccupation with the health of his soul and on the other by Luther's preoccupation with justification. Where Anselm is distinctive and interesting, however, is in the way he broadens the tradition. Here the aesthetic dimensions of his thought strengthen rather than weaken it. The effects can be seen in his doctrine of sin which is, in the first instance, conceived in largely personal and legal terms. It is an offence against what can be called rather crudely God's moral sense. But it is not so because God is understood anthropomorphically, as the criticisms of Anselm often suppose, as a rather testy monarch punishing offences against his personal honour. Sin has to be punished or atoned for in some other way because it is that which disrupts the order and beauty of the universe. It is not God but the creature who suffers as the result of sin: 'when it does not will what it ought, it dishonours God, *so far as it is concerned...* but disturbs the order and beauty of the universe... although of course it cannot injure or stain the power and dignity of God' (I,xv, my italics).

It has become fashionable in recent times to attack the doctrine of the impassibility of God, but in this context it proves its value. Sin is not a personal affront to an anthropomorphically conceived deity; because he is impassible, he cannot be harmed, let alone offended by it. We are therefore able to understand it more broadly, in a way parallel to the concept developed in Chapter 3, as personal offence indeed, and therefore as disruptive of the relation between creature and creator, but as more than that. Even here, although the process of thought begins with a legal metaphor, the argument leads us to see that it is more than simply a legal matter, but has to do with life lived in the world as a whole. And as with sin, correlatively with salvation: if sin is cosmic disorder, then salvation is the action of God as he takes responsibility for the whole context of our lives, setting us free to live in the universe he does not allow to go to ruin. Anselm may concentrate more than we should now wish on sin as offence and salvation as remission of penalty. What is significant, however, is that the way in which he sets out the problem takes us beyond the limits of his own discussion and into a further development of our theme.

IV   The Justice of God

The topic that Anselm has enabled us to approach is not only of great moment and complexity, but of almost universal religious and human interest. It has also been much neglected in recent times, and so is best approached with the help of the past, beginning with Plato. The *Republic* was devoted, in face of contemporary cynicism and relativism, to the discovery of objective moral and political realities. They were times very like our own, and in reply to those who claimed that 'justice' or political order was merely the fruit of convention or a reflection of the realities of the human struggle for power, Plato sought to show that a stable polity could be built only on the basis of the deep metaphysical structures of the universe. There is little doubt that many of the details of his programme reflect his own political pessimism and are rather reactionary and authoritarian in form. But there is one feature which is of immense importance, and that is his attempt to ground social institutions in the way the universe actually is. For Plato, the fundamental reality of things was to be found in the forms, eternal patterns or archetypes from which such order as there is in material reality takes its shape. Those worldly realities which most nearly instantiate the eternal forms will be those which are most enduring and effective. Correspondingly, the further things decline from the ideal, the worse they will be. *Justice* will be that state of affairs which prevails when social order most nearly reflects the form of justice, that is to say, when citizens co-operatively perform their proper functions. Tyranny and mob rule are the most chaotic and degenerate forms of polity because they are furthest from the eternal archetype. There is social order when the order of the universe is reflected, disorder when it is not.

It is instructive to realise that although the details and manner of Plato's programme were unique, their fundamental preoccupation was not. Hugh Lloyd-Jones' *The Justice of Zeus* is an account of how Greek culture before Plato reflects a tradition of belief about the universal basis of human fate and activity. Zeus, the chief of the gods of Olympus, represents cosmic order in a way similar to that in which Anselm's God was later to do. Lloyd-Jones' argument is that from Homer through Herodotus and the supposedly sceptical Thucydides and Euripides there is a common basic doctrine. It is that although part of the

meaning of the word *dikē* is *justice* in the sense we are used to
– of fairness in retribution and distribution in human legal
systems – it also denoted 'the preservation of the established
order' (Lloyd-Jones 1971 p.4). Indeed, the latter meaning is
the primary and determinative one. '*Dikē* means basically
the order of the universe, and in this religion the gods
maintain a cosmic order' (p.161). In Herodotus, for example, the gods maintain the order of the universe by punishing
mortals who either offend against each other or infringe
their (the gods') own prerogatives (p.59). In Aeschylus,
when the function of the Furies is transferred to the
Athenian court of the Areopagus, the point is being made
that the Athenian state now bears responsibility for the
punitive justice over which the Furies preside. 'When the
Erinyes become Eumenides, there is not the least question
of their giving up their function; we have been assured that if
they did the government both of the state and of the universe
would collapse' (p.94). Once again, human justice only
exists if it is grounded in the structure of things. A similar
point is made about the place of the sometimes derided *deus
ex machina* in the plays of Euripides. It is often held that it is
a device which is used only to get the play out of an
otherwise unavoidable impasse. In a sense that is true, but as
Lloyd–Jones points out, it is not a mere device. Human
affairs do lead into culs-de-sac. The *deus ex machina* is in
continuity with 'the Greek tradition of a divine participation in the affairs of men. The god's command helps to
bring about a restoration of the order of the universe' (p.155).

Three points of theological importance arise from that
account. The first is that although we find here the basis for a
conversation between Hellenism and Christianity, the two
traditions are not different in the way that is sometimes
supposed. It is sometimes held that the modern assertion,
inspired by the Enlightenment, of human autonomy against

any form of heteronomy is a reassertion of Greek values against the Christian tradition. There is something in the claim, but it can only be made, according to Lloyd-Jones, by being very selective with the evidence. '(W)hatever the generous sympathies of liberals like Shelley may lead them to imagine, Prometheus is only a minor figure in the Greek pantheon. Not Prometheus but Zeus is the ruler of the universe' (p.103). The debate between Athens and Jerusalem is therefore not, in this context at any rate, as simple as is sometimes supposed. It is not a simple debate between autonomy and heteronomy, progressive and conservative, but between both ancient traditions and a certain form of modernism. The two traditions, as they are represented in such figures as those providing Lloyd-Jones' materials and the Christian Anselm, share a view that the universe has an order which is maintained by Zeus and the triune God alike. Where they differ, and this is the second point, is in the manner and character of the order. Lloyd-Jones sees the difference to be between an essentially immanent order, for the Greek gods are thus conceived to operate, and one which works 'by means of extraneous interventions' (p.162), a view he presumably takes to be the Christian one. Anselm's theology would give him some supporting evidence, for it does reveal a relative failure to link the incarnation with creation and human regeneration. But, third, an even more important difference is to be found elsewhere. The justice of Zeus, as manifest in the literature of classical Greece, is 'that "violent grace" by virtue of which he punishes, late or soon, a man who has done injustice to another, either in his own person or in that of his descendants' (p.161). Anselm's God, in almost total contrast, although he too is responsible for the good order of the universe, operates not by punishing but by mercifully accepting the gift of infinite value given on behalf of the offender by the God–man.

Both traditions, accordingly, are concerned with justice in its cosmic as well as its personal dimensions. But their means of attaining it are opposite. In some ways, it must be confessed, Anselm's God comes off worse, because it is possible for the unsympathetic to see in his work a mere 'transaction', a legal fiction almost, by which a just penalty is avoided – what Edward Irving, referring not, it is to be hoped, to Anselm but to second rate successors, called a 'stock-exchange divinity'. By contrast, the Greek tradition represents a kind of common sense view of things, in which the function of the gods is to see that wickedness is punished.

V Justice, Justification, Judgement

The comparison between two traditions of thought reveals something of the importance of the concept of the justice of God in the history of thought. The contrast between them reveals at the same time why it has been possible for there to be a perpetual debate between two general possibilities for understanding the nature of the world. There is a real clash between Athens and Jerusalem, and it comes to a famous encounter in some oft-quoted words of Martin Luther:

> For I hated that word 'righteousness of God', which, according to the use and custom of all the teachers, I had been taught to understand philosophically regarding the formal or active righteousness... with which God is righteous and punishes the unrighteous sinner... I began to understand that the righteousness of God is that by which the righteous lives by a gift of God... the passive righteousness with which merciful God justifies us by faith. (Luther 1545/1960 p.336)

At the heart of that passage is a repetition of the contrary views of Greece and Anselm as they came into view in the previous section. It also encapsulates part of the difference between Christianity and paganism, as well as between

Christianity as it was reshaped at the Reformation and the modern cult of autonomy. The Christian church still stands or falls by whether it proclaims and lives by the gospel of the liberating grace of God, or whether its life degenerates into some form of self-salvation. For that reason, the doctrine of the atonement must continue to be at the heart of Christian theology, and the metaphor of the justice of God at the heart of the doctrine of the atonement, if Christianity's orientation to the action of God in re-establishing free human life is to be maintained and articulated.

It is also true, however, that Luther formulated the matter in a rather one-sided way. His conception of justification, dominated as it was by features of his personal experience as well as by the Western church's Augustinian heritage, led to the neglect of some of the features we have seen to be important. The meaning of the justice of God, so closely linked with justification, came to be too closely tied to individual sin and forgiveness, too loosely to the cosmic and social dimensions which have been a part of other developments of the subject. The chief point, however, is not to apportion blame for the development so much as to realise what has happened since then. The increasingly subjective turn of the modern mind has meant that treatments of the human plight and its healing have taken an increasingly inward and individualistic direction, as the thought of two modern heirs of Luther, Kierkegaard and Bultmann, demonstrates clearly. Some forms of pietism and mysticism illustrate the same trend. In another and related direction, excessive preoccupation with the juridical aspects of the doctrine of justification has led to versions of penal substitution which do appear to attribute to God an excessively punitive character. So much hangs on a sensitive appreciation of what are the possibilities and limits of the legal metaphor.

It is, therefore, essential to return to the biblical foun-
tainhead of the matter, and to look briefly at what Paul, as
the source of Luther's claims, had to say. There is a sense in
which the Letter to the Romans can be interpreted as a
treatise on the justice of God. When it is looked at as a
whole, however, it becomes clear that it is a mistake to
interpret the legal metaphor in a narrowly personalistic or
individualistic way. The centre is undoubtedly the justification of sinners, but they are seen in the context of a world
which stands or falls with them. The opening chapter
illustrates that theme, for it construes human fallenness in
terms not only of particular patterns of sinful behaviour but
also of a decline into the moral and physical slavery which
results from the worship and service of the creature instead
of the Creator (Rom. 1.22-25). Having expounded in the
first seven chapters the nature of the human plight and its
healing, employing legal but also sacrificial metaphors, Paul
returns in chapter 8 to the place where justification is to be
lived out, the created order as a whole. The justifying Spirit
anticipates and portends the ultimate liberation of the
creation itself from its bondage to decay (8.19-23). The
justice of God, that is to say, is the form of God's action in
saving human beings in and with the cosmos. As the book
proceeds, other cognate themes come to the fore. In
chapters 9-11 Paul tackles the question of how history
demonstrates the outworking of the divine justice, seeking
to show that the election of Israel continues to be the means
by which the salvation of the whole world is to take place.
Then in the final chapters, which are largely concerned with
Christian behaviour, he moves to the living out of the justice
of God in daily life. The justification of the sinner, then, is
only a part of what is meant by the justice of God, which is
conceived more broadly in terms of the transformation of

the whole created order, as the outcome – as we shall see – of God's loyalty to his creation.

If we look back, so to speak, at the Old Testament background to Paul's theology, we shall find confirmation of this broader meaning of the concept. There is, of course, much concern with law and justice in the narrower sense: not so much in Anselm's rather Romanised concept of giving to God what is his due, but in a more covenantal context. God's law is given, as the prophets reminded Israel, to regulate relationships within the covenant community, especially where the poor and defenceless are concerned. God is just because he sees to it that there is a structure provided within which his people may order their lives without fear and in freedom. But that narrower sense does not encompass the whole. In a recent review of German scholarly discussion of 'God's righteousness', M.T. Brauch makes three observations which are particularly relevant to the theme of this chapter. The first is that although Luther himself conceived justice as creative and redemptive activity, his contemporaries and successors tended to lapse back into a pre-Reformation understanding of justice as merely distributive (Brauch 1977 pp.523ff). The second is that although there is some disagreement among recent scholars, many now see, with the help of the Old Testament, that an important aspect of the concept's meaning centres on the notion of God's faithfulness to his entire creation (pp.528,531). We have already seen something of this in connection with Paul's theology, but it is worth noting that something of it reappears in Anselm's belief (see above, section II) that the incarnation took place in order that God should complete what he began in creating the human race, as well as in Athanasius' more universal 'it were not worthy of God's goodness that the things he had made should waste away' (*De Inc.* 6). On a broad conception of the justice of

God such as this, we are able to avoid a conception of the atonement which restricts it to an 'intervention' of God in history for narrowly moralistic reasons and to understand it as the outcome of the love and goodness of God which he bears eternally to the whole of creation.

The third point made by Brauch in his survey is that several scholars see justice as a relational concept, to be understood against the background of the covenant relationship of God with Israel. In the New Testament, however, it has a meaning far beyond the notion of God's covenant faithfulness to his people: in Paul it refers to God's eschatological, recreating power, in which the sinner is taken up into a new relationship by the grace of God. The point about justice being a relational concept is very important, and worth developing, for it emphasises that justice is not a *state* but something that takes place between God and the world or between people. Something of what it means in Romans is brought out by E.P. Sanders, who notes, first, the variety of uses of the concept, indicating as it does God's power, action, rightness and fidelity (Sanders 1977 p.491). Sanders also shows an awareness of the metaphorical nature of the language, for he says that although Paul is not primarily concerned with juristic categories, he does work with them (p.502). What he finds is a combination of juristic and what he calls participationist categories. Both aspects are important. The language is used in a participationist way because it is concerned with the relation of believers to Christ, and so helps to avoid a merely external or legalistic interpretation of salvation. Justification is not a legal fiction but a new relationship. The juristic connotations, however, continue to have a part to play, because they prevent Paul from lapsing into antinomianism – for justice in the narrower sense matters – or into ahistorical forms of piety (p.520).

With the help of these scholarly discoveries we are enabled to see metaphor at work, giving Paul at once a rooting in a tradition of language and the flexibility to change it in order to do justice to new realities. Drawing upon Old Testament and other sources, he moulds a family of words into vehicles by which the meaning of the cross is made known. It is worth mentioning again that he does not expect one set of metaphors to do all the work. Just as in the discussion of victory we found ourselves ineluctably led into the legal sphere, so here Paul cannot teach justification without appealing also to the imagery of sacrifice: 'they are justified through his grace as a gift, through the redemption which is in Christ Jesus, whom God put forward as an expiation by his blood, to be received by faith' (Rom.3.24f). Thus do the metaphors converge and combine as their users attempt to express the meaning of different aspects of the atonement.

VI   Two Twentieth Century Theologies

The metaphors with which we are concerned in this book have the importance that they do because they help to articulate a central feature of the human condition. It is for that reason that they are finally unfathomable and present to the theologian ever new possibilities for insight and development. For the same reason, no final account can be given of what they mean, certainly not this side of eternity: they are eschatological concepts, giving up their secrets only by anticipation and through the gift of the Spirit. We shall not therefore expect the classical theologies of the atonement to be finally adequate, and shall avoid using the word 'theories' of them, certainly if that suggests that there are fixed meanings to them that can be played off against each other. Two points must therefore be made at this stage of the discussion of the justice of God. Looking back we must say that there is much to be learned from Anselm and Luther, despite the much rehearsed weaknesses of their formulations, simply because they are classic articulations of the human condition before God. But surveying our own times, we can also be aware that there have in recent times been two great expressions of this aspect of the atonement, different from each other and yet bringing to our attention important developments of the metaphor.

The first is P.T. Forsyth's *The Justification of God*, which was a response to the moral catastrophe of the First World War. It is, as the title suggests, a theodicy, an attempt to 'justify the ways of God to Men'. Interestingly, its approach is nearer to that of Milton than to modern discussions of what has come to be called the problem of evil. Forsyth argues for the justice of God not by attempting to establish the conceptual compatibility of God's omnipotence and goodness (see Surin 1986), but by showing how God deals with evil historically and in practice. The theme of the book is that the justice of God can be found only where he justifies himself, and that is in the act of atonement on the cross. Forsyth shares with Anselm the concern to allow the metaphor of justice to take shape, to be filled with its proper meaning, at the place where God takes upon himself the evil for which he is held responsible (Forsyth 1916 p.125). And so, like Anselm, but in a different way, he moves away from looking at the matter juristically, merely in terms of law, and treats the matter as a metaphor for aspects of the personal relations of God and humankind. 'The cross is not a theological theme, nor a forensic device, but the crisis of the moral universe on a scale far greater than earthly war. It is the theodicy of the whole God dealing with the whole soul of the whole world in holy love, righteous judgement and redeeming grace' (p.136). Again and again Forsyth turns the attention of the reader to the cross as the action of God which bears on life as a whole rather than being the legal transaction that it has sometimes been made to appear. He thus seeks to allow that about which he is speaking to shape the language he uses, so that the language may make real the divine–human relationship which is its concern. Forsyth is sometimes held to be stronger on rhetoric than on careful analysis, but his detailed working out of his theme shows how germane is his development to the theme of this chapter.

First of all, it must be said that he shows an awareness of what we have already found to be at the heart of our conversation on the traditions, that there is a link between matters of justice more narrowly conceived and the created order as a whole. Forsyth refuses to think deistically of the relation between God and the world, but sees them in intimate and dynamic interaction. 'Our deeper views of creation... do not allow us to think of the universe as an external and mechanical product... The existence of the universe is too closely bound up with the being of God for that. Its life is the immanence of the Transcendent' (p.73). For that reason, he holds, we must understand the atonement as the renewal of the life of the creation, far more, that is, than some past transaction. 'The curse of orthodoxy... has been to sever the cross from the whole moral fabric and movement of the universe and make it a theologian's affair' (p.192). Rather, Forsyth wants us to see the cross as a way to express theologically a living relation between God and the world. There he shows his kinship with theologians like Irenaeus and, indeed, for all his sideswipes at orthodoxy, Anselm.

And yet, secondly, Forsyth's use of *justice* remains metaphorical in the further sense of retaining its link with more ordinary uses of the term. It is a matter of justice in a more restricted sense as well, because for Forsyth the collapse of civilised Europe into a barbarous war derived from a breakdown of human morality. Therefore he will not separate the doctrine of the atonement from what he calls the 'righteousness in things' (p.161). Salvation is bound up with judgement, which therefore forbids any Christian talk of reconciliation from collapsing into a sentimentality that ignores moral right and wrong. The cross shows us that the Great War is a divine judgement on human wickedness. 'The idea of a judgement is bound up with a moral order of a very real, immanent, and urgent, not to say eternal, kind.' Therefore 'grace, acting by way of atonement, has in its very nature a moral element, which does not leave the indifferent immune... Judgment is the negative side of love's positive righteousness' (p.186). It is a function of the justice realised on the cross to lay bare the sinfulness of human behaviour.

The third feature brings us to what is most distinctively modern about Forsyth's treatment of our topic, and is best brought out by another reference to the justice of Zeus and that of Anselm's God. According to Lloyd-Jones, the Greek concept centred on the fact that the justice of God was something that operated immanently, within the order of things, to punish the guilty, and, as we have seen, he believes this to distinguish Hellenism from Christianity. For Anselm, on the other hand, God is conceived as transcendent, as other than the world, but as providing through the incarnation (the Son's immanence in history) the means of forgiveness. At first sight, the difference between the Greek and the Christian is that between punishment and forgiveness, vengeance and mercy and there is much in that.[3] Forsyth, however, enables us to see that the matter is much more complex. There is an immanent judgement, in that indeed the vice and blindness of nations bring them

3. See below Chapter 7, Section V for the recurring charge against Christianity on this count.

ineluctibly to disaster. We cannot leave out of account the insights of the Greek tragedians who saw, and saw clearly, so much about the human predicament. Here the Greek and the Christian have much in common. The difference between them lies, rather, in the way in which the justice of God is seen to operate *within the order of things*. Forsyth's crucial advance is to bring to the fore – although it was not completely absent from Anselm – the sovereign freedom of God. 'God's justification of man... was by His justification of Himself in man' (p.174). The justice of God, accordingly, lies not in some device whereby the unforgiveable could be forgiven, but in the action by which God provides – immanently, within human history – the means of moral regeneration. The cross is at once 'the solution and the destruction of the world's moral anomalies' not because it harmonises (abstract) justice and mercy, but because as 'the creative focus of the moral world' it is 'the rightful and the real ruler of the course of history'(p.106). It is God's way of so relating himself to human history that new relationships are made both possible and real.

The chief weakness of an account such as Forsyth's is that it may appear to lack a grounding in actual human life, but that is a topic for a later chapter. At this stage, the enquiry is concerned to show how the metaphor of the justice of God can in general be shown to make sense, and in that respect much can be learned from *The Justification of God*. Especially when it is viewed with eyes given us by the other authorities of this chapter, it enables us to see how the concept can function in modern conditions. The possibilities are extended when we turn from Forsyth's to Barth's treatment of the legal metaphor, 'The Judge Judged in our Place' (Barth 1953/1956 pp.211-83). That title immediately suggests, with its use of imagery evoking the thought that the judge steps into the dock in place of the accused, a more directly juridical use of language. But the claim that the one who has the right to be our judge does not behave in the way expected of judges brings in its train a considerable change of meaning. The heart of the change is the development by which 'to judge' is understood to be the equivalent of 'standing in judgement', so that the concept is, so to speak, personalized: used of personal relations rather than of a legal process. Once again, we find the centre of interest not some legal transaction but the way God acts toward us.

That section of Barth's *Church Dogmatics* has to be understood in the context of Volume IV as a whole. In it, the atonement – or reconciliation as Barth prefers to call it[4] – is understood as the threefold action of God's self-humbling, humankind's elevation to true humanity and the mediating action of Jesus Christ as both God and man. In our section, Barth argues that God exercises his function of judgement by taking to himself 'the lost cause of man' (p.3). That human lostness is itself understood in terms of the primary metaphor to mean that, after the manner of Adam in Genesis 3, 'man wants to be his own judge' (p.220). We stand in judgement on our neighbour in the attitude which for Barth encapsulates human sinfulness. We want to be 'godlike' and to convince ourselves that we are in the right and everybody else in the wrong. In response to our demonic self-divinisation God refuses to exercise a like judgement of superiority, but instead himself undergoes the judicial process. But just as our victories are really defeats and God's defeat on the cross really a victory, so it is here. The refusal

---

4. As R.S. Paul shows (1961 pp.20ff), the English words *reconcile* and *atone* have been for part of their history virtual synonyms. The latter therefore need not necessarily bear all of the connotations it has sometimes gathered.

to exercise judgement is the way by which the judge of all
things does effect his righteous rule.

How is this exercise of divine judgement to be understood? First of all, by means of an apparent paradox: 'to
show His grace in the execution of His judgement, to
pronounce us free in passing sentence, to free us by
imprisoning us, to ground our life on our death, to redeem
and save us by our own destruction' (p.222). The paradox,
however is resolved in a twofold way by, so to speak,
unpacking and expounding the metaphor. We have already
seen that one of the functions of metaphor is to reveal
hidden features of the human condition by carrying over
meaning from one sphere of reality to another, and so it is
here. To understand the cross as a judgement is to hold that
just as a court decides and so declares a verdict of guilt, so the
cross lays bare certain aspects of our condition – for
example, the pride of our standing in judgement on others.
But it is not simply a matter of showing something to be so.
Because it is the action of the eternal Son become man, it is
also a redemptive action taking place at the heart of our
lostness:

> The 'for us' of His death on the cross includes and
> encloses this terrible 'against us'. Without this terrible
> 'against us' it would not be the divine and holy and
> redemptive and effectively helpful 'for us' in which the
> conversion of man and the world to God has become
> an event. (p.296)

The judgement of which Barth speaks is a kind of death
sentence, the metaphorical *but real* execution of the sinner:

> For the fact that God has given Himself in His Son to
> suffer the divine judgement on us men does not mean
> that it is not executed on us, but that it is executed on
> us... That Jesus Christ died for us does not mean,
> therefore, that we do not have to die, but that we have

died in and with Him, that as the people we were we
have been done away with and destroyed. (pp.294f)
God exercises his justice by revealing our sin, by bearing it
and by destroying its power. Like Forsyth, Barth may at
times appear to be stronger on rhetoric than in concretely
setting out the way by which the justice of God becomes real
in human life. Again, however, it must be remembered that
we are here concerned primarily with what he does conceptually with a metaphor of atonement. It is the action of
creating a variation on a conceptual theme that Anselm,
Luther, Forsyth and Barth have in common, despite differences in the way they 'cash' the central metaphor. All
alike articulate their theologies in such a way as to show the
centrality of the metaphor to the Christian analysis of the
human condition and God's saving action in relation to it.
When compared with Lloyd-Jones, however, they reveal
two more important features. The first is that it is not simply
a Christian metaphor, but one that appears to articulate a
basic and widespread, possibly universal, human response
to the universe. The second is that a Christian theology
centred on the atonement presents a radically different
conception from that of the Greeks both of what it is to be
human and of the way in which God is conceived to uphold
the justice of the universe.

The argument of this chapter, therefore, has shown that it
is possible to speak of a conversation between two chief
ways of using the metaphor of the justice of God; and within
that of variations on the way in which the metaphor may be
developed in Christian theology. At this stage, we are not
yet concerned to do full justice to the metaphors by
developing a systematic account of the ways in which they
may still be used after the criticisms which the doctrines
enshrined in them have received in recent times. What is
being claimed is that these ways of speaking cannot be

dismissed as being without meaning, or as being mere pictures. They have articulated and continue to articulate in writings up to the present day a way of speaking about life in the world: its nature, its fallenness and its redemption. The Christian writers in particular live from a conception of the relationship of God to the world which is to be found in Paul's theology of the cross in particular. The cross is the place where God provides the means of the free forgiveness and sanctification of the sinner without implying that the universe is an unjust place and that he is indifferent to moral realities: he is at once just and justifies the sinner. The heart of the matter is the use of the metaphor: that a concept whose apparently primary meaning is to be found in matters of legality is now used chiefly to explicate relationships between persons, and in particular the all determining relationship between the creator and his erring but never abandoned children. In that respect, the same kind of thing has been found as in the previous chapter: that a metaphor or family of metaphors takes its shape from the divine and human story it seeks to narrate, and so enables aspects of the meaning of an unfathomable mystery to be expressed in language.

5

Christ the Sacrifice: a Dead Metaphor?

Will all great Neptune's ocean wash this blood
Clean from my hands? No, this hand will rather
The multitudinous seas incarnadine
Making the green one red.
Shakespeare, Macbeth, II.ii.59

I   The Problem

It is not difficult to conceive that the metaphors of victory and justice could appeal to the modern mind. Both are concepts in everyday use, and the questions of what it is to win a victory or to seek and obtain justice are real ones. With sacrifice, the currency of the imagery is much more questionable, as J.S. Whale pointed out some time ago.

In our modern world sacrifice has become a mere figure of speech. Parents sacrifice themselves for their children; a politician may sacrifice a career for a principle...

In the ancient world sacrifice was no figure of speech but stark fact; the solemn taking and surrendering of the warm blood of life itself; the ritual slaughter of bullock or goat, lamb or pigeon at an altar. It asserted the powerful religious efficacy of shed blood. Ancient man took the necessity of blood sacrifice for granted. Indeed, sacrifice is as ancient and universal as religion itself; it expresses the ultimate concern of the human race.

But modern man finds the very idea revolting, on more than one ground. (Whale 1960 p.42)

That passage asserts that *sacrifice*, while still a ('mere') figure of speech, has for the most part ceased to be a living metaphor. If, then, it has become not merely a dead but a debased metaphor, is it possible any longer to use it in connection with the real world with which we are concerned, with God and his saving action? Can we any more cut the world at its joints with its assistance? The question for this chapter is whether the loss is total, or whether the problem is as much ours as that of the language.

To the problem of the debasement of language there is added the fact, also alluded to in the passage from Whale, that the idea is now found to be 'revolting'. There are two aspects to the dissatisfaction which is very much a feature of the Western world after the Enlightenment. The first is a consideration often advanced in nineteenth century discussions of the matter, that the language of sacrifice belongs to features of the Old Testament cult that have been superseded by more directly ethical Christian concerns. We shall see later that such an objection misunderstands the relation between Christianity and its Jewish basis. The second ground of dissatisfaction is to be found in the fact that sacrifice gains much of its meaning from the shedding of blood which it involves. A mixture of perplexity and horror greeted a recent reported animal sacrifice in the suburbs of London, revealing the complete alienation of the Western mind from this ancient institution. Add to that the widespread belief that so to interpret the death of Jesus is to suggest that in some way God demands the blood of an innocent victim before he will enter into relation with his people, and we can well understand the difficulty we face. Can an analysis of sacrifice as metaphor begin to remove so deep a resistance to the idea?

A preliminary general point to be made is that this account of the modern consciousness has somewhat oversimplified the matter. If we turn to the evidence of English literature, for example, it becomes evident that the notion of sacrifice sometimes operates as far more than a dead metaphor. In Frances Young's *Sacrifice and the Death of Christ* allusion is made to two modern novels, Steinbeck's *To a God Unknown* and Golding's *Lord of the Flies,* both of which, by their depictions of apparently archaic responses to reality, 'may enable us to enter more sympathetically into the culture of the ancient world... But they may do more than this. They may help us to rediscover certain basic human responses and reactions' (Young 1975 pp.15f). That is useful, as far as it goes. The claim is that there is something inherent in the human constitution from which the phenomenon of sacrifice derives and to which it continues to appeal. Perhaps, then, it could be said that the debased survivals to which Whale refers retain their limited currency because they appeal to something innate in the human spirit?

Studies of the phenomenon in the ancient world, however, show that such is only a beginning. If we are to demonstrate that the modern novels do not simply represent atavistic survivals from the past, to be finally expunged when enlightenment is complete, we have to probe more deeply into the meaning of the institution in human culture. If we do, we shall realise that sacrifice has to do not simply with human subjectivity or social custom, but – and here we meet again a familiar theme – with those in their wider environment. Here, if we are to understand the springs of what is sometimes called, with patronising overtones, primitive religion, we must beware of assumptions of the superiority of contemporary enlightenment. As Mary Douglas has argued, we may assume neither the intellectual immaturity of earlier cultures nor the axiomatic maturity of our own. In certain respects, 'primitives' have the advantage over us, for 'in the primitive culture the rule of patterning works with greater force and more total comprehensiveness. With the moderns, it applies to disjointed, separate areas of existence' (Douglas 1984 p.40). The ancients see things whole in a way that we moderns, with our fragmented experience, often fail to.

In her book, Professor Douglas is speaking chiefly of purity and defilement rather than directly of sacrifice, but the relevance is clear. Ancient and modern ideas of purity are, like ancient notions of sacrifice, concerned with certain dimensions of human living in the world. Far from being a symptom of the irrationality of the primitive, the desire to see things whole betokens a concern for the order of creation. Mary Douglas believes that it was because of their narrowly modernist conception of rationality that Old Testament scholars long failed to realise the rationale of the classifications of clean and unclean beasts in the book of Leviticus, with the result that they were either confounded by them, or dismissive of the mentality that could devise so apparently pointless a scheme. The key to the distinction is, however, there to be found: 'Holiness means keeping distinct the categories of creation. It therefore involves correct definition, discrimination and order' (p.53). The unclean beasts are those that in some way appear to violate the due order of things. The point here is not that we should necessarily find the classification convincing, but that we should realise that it has to do with order, which means in this context wholeness or completeness, particularly in relation to God. Sacrifice is the other side of the matter, and has to do at least in part with the ordering and reordering of life both in the cosmos and in relation to God. We may now be bound to use the word metaphorically, but this need not be at the expense of these important considerations. There is a continuity of meaning to be found, and it is in the universal human desire that life in the world be whole and good.

Corresponding to the desire for wholeness is an equivalent conception of disorder. We have met in previous chapters two theologies of sin which are, so to speak, the shadows cast by the light of salvation. In the light of the teaching that the cross is a victory, sin is conceived as a bondage from which only God in Christ can set us free. The other side of the teaching that God justifies the sinner is the fact that sin can be understood as the breach of the law. So, here, sin is construed in terms of uncleanness. 'Deep in the heart of mankind there is an instinctive aversion to dirt, disease and death, and in almost every language the words which convey this abhorrence are used metaphorically to express and evoke a similar loathing for sin, and especially for sins of fraud, sensuality and violence' (Caird 1980 p.17). In this respect, Greek (see Parker 1984) and Hebrew cultures were similar, even though deep differences on the nature of *miasma* and its removal remained. Professor Douglas points out that modern patterns of behaviour are equivalent, even though we often suppose that our preoccupation with hygiene is purely rational (pp.29-40). More pertinent to the fact that it is sin we are talking about is the often remarked fact that those who commit rape are often motivated by a desire to defile and pollute those whom they violate. Undoubtedly, when we speak of these matters we are by no means in the realm of survivals of quaint institutions from primitive ages.

We shall, accordingly, begin to understand the nature of sacrifice when we come to see its function in the removal of the uncleanness which pollutes the good creation. That may be the reason why sacrifice is apparently a universal or near universal (see Sykes 1980 p.61) feature of human behaviour. I do not want to suggest that this is its only meaning, and the argument of the rest of the chapter will give reasons why it is not. The purpose of this section is rather to provide a purchase on the topic and to suggest that we are here in a region of widespread if not universal human responses to the world. A feeling of the rightness or even necessity of a sacrificial dimension to our existence runs very deep in human experience. Such a consideration, however, takes us only a short way. It could still be argued that the vestiges of sacrificial imagery in our languages are no more than an atavistic survival, the last remains of primitive consciousness. Or it may be dismissed on the theological grounds that have already been mentioned, as a mythological projection, to be expunged by the pure milk of a truly ethical gospel. Before it can be shown that the death of Christ ought to be described as a sacrifice, there is much more to be done.

II   The Bible and the Metaphor

The original literal meaning of the word *sacrifice* is to be found in the institution by which a living being is ritually slaughtered for some social or religious end. Instances of the sacrifice of human beings are to be found in Greek history but only very rarely in Hebrew religion, so that the Old Testament practice with which we begin is centred on the slaughter of animals or the gift of some inanimate substitute.[1] Biblical sacrifices were made for various purposes: for sin, for the sealing of a covenant, for thanksgiving, for the remembrance of a historic salvation, for communion with God, or simply as a gift in response to God's goodness. There is much dispute in the literature about the details of some of these matters, whose interpretation is by no means

1. The latter is very important in demonstrating, as Whale points out, that sacrifice does not here carry any connotations of vengeance or punishment: 'You cannot punish a cupful of barley' (Whale 1960 p.53).

agreed. But for our purposes the chief point is that there is in the Old Testament a great variety of practice and interpretation which is in turn reflected in the variety of free use made of the available imagery in New Testament thought about the significance of Jesus. One unifying feature is indicated by John Rogerson: 'ultimately, all sacrifices in the Old Testament depend for their context upon the story of God's deliverance of his people from Egypt at the Exodus' (Rogerson 1980 p.57). If there is a single centre, it is to be found at the place where Israel began to understand the roots of her life in its relation to God.

That point leads immediately to another. Because we are concerned with so various and widespread a practice, we should be careful not to assume that it will always have the same meaning. When different cultures and religions do the same *kind* of thing – ritually slaughtering animals – they are not necessarily doing the *same* thing. The contexts affect, perhaps sometimes determine, the meaning. Even when the expression of the matter appears quite similar, as when the Homeric gods enjoy the smoke of the heroes' holocaust and 'the Lord smelled the pleasing savour' of Noah's sacrifice (Gen.8.21), the particular and general contexts indicate that we are whole worlds apart in the meaning given to the institution. Or, to take another example, it is one thing to sacrifice a daughter in order to win a fair wind to set sail for war, another to sacrifice one in fulfilment of a rash promise. Such a consideration reminds us that we must always remember that language is flexible rather than rigid, and that in turn leads us back to the matter of metaphor.

The use of the term *sacrifice* in a metaphorical way begins already in the Old Testament. This is an absolutely crucial fact for us to bear in mind if we are to make sense of later developments. 'The sacrifice acceptable to God is a broken spirit...' (Ps.51.17, cf 27.6 and 107.22). A further interesting fact is that, whether or not some of the prophets, on grounds such as these, rejected the sacrificial cult completely, as a straightforward reading of their words would suggest (see, for example, Amos 5.21ff), the cult continued, so that literal and metaphorical meanings continued side by side: sacrifice was *both* slaughter and prayer. The duality is repeated at a different level in the New Testament, which can, first, speak of the death of Christ as a sacrifice, for example in Heb.9.26c: '(Christ) has appeared at the end of the age to put away sin by the sacifice of himself.' This is clearly a metaphorical use of language: there is no altar, but a cross; he is killed by soldiers not (directly – see John 11.50) by priests; and there is no provision in the sacrificial regulations as they appear in the canon of the Old Testament for the sacrifice of a human victim. Therefore, the death is described with the help of a true metaphor, for it both is and is not a sacrifice. The metaphorical use of language is indicated also in the free use which the writers make of the different aspects of Old Testament practice and interpretation. Thus the writer to the Hebrews appears to conflate different aspects of the Day of Atonement ritual from Leviticus 16, and the Fourth Gospel combines passover and sin offerings in its interpretation of the life and passion of Jesus. As Frances Young shows, different strands of the Old Testament language of sacrifice are applied to Jesus in different ways. That is archetypally metaphorical, as it involves what Aristotle saw as the heart of metaphor, the transfer of language from one context to another.

But, second, the metaphorical way in which Jesus is described as a sacrifice itself becomes the basis of a further metaphor. One of the central aspects of the 'standard' usage, its involvement with a death, drops away, and believers are recommended, in dependence on the one sacrifice of Jesus Christ, to 'present your bodies as a living sacrifice' (Rom.

12.1). The sacrifice of Christ is metaphorical not in the sense that it is unreal, for it really is a sacrifice, but in the sense we have noted; that of the believer, in that the mode of life enjoined is transferred both linguistically and as a matter of living practice from the primary sacrifice on which the manner of life depends. That is to say, we *understand* from the life and death of Jesus what a sacrifice really is; and we *receive* from him the means of living the kind of life that is set forth in the narratives and other forms of speech about him.

Our chief concern here, however, is with the dominant New Testament metaphor – the description of the life and death of Jesus as a sacrifice – and with what it enables us to say about the meaning of Jesus, and, consequently, the nature of God and life in the world. In what ways does this metaphor clear the sight for new vision? The first way is one that has often been remarked, that the centring of the new meaning of the word *sacrifice* on the death of Jesus brings it about that there is now only one sacrifice that really matters. The writer to the Hebrews, the New Testament writer most reponsible for the development of this theme, stresses the once and for all nature of the sacrifice (7.27), and the implication that it removes the necessity for a repeated blood sacrifice. It did not take long for that to become a commonplace in Christian teaching. What is also worth noting is that the critique of animal sacrifice that followed logically from it may be one of the reasons why the notion of blood sacrifice has become so objectionable to the modern mind. The story of Jesus teaches us that sacrifice of this kind is no longer relevant to divine-human relations. 'For it is impossible that the blood of bulls and goats should take away sins' (Heb.10.14). Hebrews is in part a moral critique, based on that Psalm 40.6-8. The metaphorical sacrifice has done what no repeated animal sacrifice can do, 'purify your conscience from dead works to serve the living God' (Heb.9.14). How it may be understood that the one sacrifice has made all the others obsolete will exercise us later; at this stage, we shall concentrate on the meaning of the metaphor, and what can be called its revelatory character.

The second major feature of the transfer of meaning is to be found in the fact that for the Letter to the Hebrews the sacrifice is also the priest. This is another quite remarkable feature of what happened under the impact of the Christian gospel. The conflation of the two ideas of sacrifice and priest is part of what can be called the moralising of the concept, so long as it is not forgotten that, despite what this epistle sometimes suggests, there was always a close link in Hebrew sacrifice between institution and ethics. Now, however, meaning comes to be centred on the fact that in his death, considered as the completion of his life, there is a gift by Jesus of *himself.* As the high priest under the old dispensation gives some kind of access to God by his actions, so this high priest, because he came from and has returned to God, 'has no need to offer sacrifices daily...; he did this once and for all, when he offered up himself' (Heb.7.27). From the Letter to the Hebrews, then, we learn particularly of what can be called the human self-giving of Jesus, the eternal Son (Heb.1.2-3) come among us as priest and sacrifice.

If, however, we are to avoid suggestions that the sacrifice of Jesus is in some way a punitive substitution, in which God punishes him for our sins, we must pay full attention to this aspect of the matter. As a sacrifice of himself, the death of Jesus was a free and voluntary human act. As we have seen, sacrifice became for some of the Psalmists a way of speaking of the true worship and form of life required by God of his people. It has also been suggested that the tradition, in speaking of the atonement, has sometimes failed to give sufficient weight to the life of Jesus in its particular humanity. Here is an opportunity to stress the importance of the human action of Jesus. His sacrifice, as the Letter to the Hebrews stresses so strongly, is not the imposed death of the beast, but the voluntary self-giving of a man. Indeed, it is more than simply voluntary: 'for the joy that was set before him (he) endured the cross, despising the shame' (Heb.12.2). Simliarly, the Epistle to the Ephesians stresses the element of worship. Jesus offers to the Father the human life that the others of us have so signally failed to live: 'Christ loved us and gave himself up for us, a fragrant offering and sacrifice to God' (Eph.5.2). Once again we find in the manner of Jesus' life, interpreted through the focus provided by a central metaphor, a concrete instance of what it is to be human. The metaphor is revealing precisely because its usage is in continuity with other ways of speaking, while at the same time startlingly new.

Only when we have given full weight to the implications of the human story for our understanding of the metaphor may we move to the third way in which new vision is created. Two chapters ago it was argued that the fullness of the metaphor of victory is lost if we do not realise that the gospel narratives depict at once a human and divine victory, and one that is only divine because it is human. So it is here. The sacrifice which is Jesus' human self-giving to God and to humankind is also and at the same time the gift of God. 'God gave his only-begotten Son' (John 3.16) is surely to be understood as an appeal to a sacrificial notion, especially in view of the fact that, as has already been suggested, this author appears to understand Jesus at once in terms of sin and passover offerings. Similarly Paul: God 'did not spare his own Son but gave him up for us all' (Rom.8.32), an expression that must surely be interpreted with the help of the sacrificial language of Rom. 3.25.[2] This is perhaps the most remarkable metaphorical transfer of them all. In most sacrificial systems, sacrifice is something people give to God: in some of them as a means by which the deity is appeased or 'bought off'; in the Bible more as a gift to the God who by virtue of who he is cannot be bought. When Christ is described as a sacrifice, the notion of gift remains, but both the nature of the giver and the means of the giving are understood very differently. The most radical aspect of the change is that there is a reversal of roles. In the Old Testament, although God is the one who provides the institution of sacrifice as part of his covenant with Israel, the sacrifice is made by and on behalf of Israel. Now, the primary giver is God, not a human priest. This is particularly evident in the Pauline writings, but it is everywhere the implicit or explicit assumption of New Testament theology. It is because we are helpless (Rom.5.6) that God has to renew by his sacrifice the covenant made at the creation and repeated in various forms in Old Testament witness. The transfer of the function of offering from finite human to eternal God would account for the appeal of Gen.22.8 for the New Testament writers: 'God will provide himself the lamb.' In the story of Abraham's sacrifice of Isaac, God's covenant with Abraham is saved and renewed when the ram is found in the thicket. So, when we are helpless God gives the means of our being restored to the covenant relationship.

What does this mean for our understanding of God? The church's worship and life takes its meaning from the confession that God himself acts to bring his people into relationship with himself. Just as our two previous meta-

2. Barrett (1962 p.172) argues that the verse alludes to Abraham's willingness to sacrifice Isaac. Whatever be the case, we have here another component in the kaleidoscope of images which together constitute the New Testament characterisation of Jesus as sacrifice.

phors were seen to be revelatory of the ways of God towards his world, so it is here. We can see a little of what it means with the help of the parable of the Prodigal Son's depiction of the behaviour of the father. Unlike Aristotle's great-souled man, who does not break into a run, this man, in his love for his lost son, cares nothing for appearance and dignity. All is sacrificed in order that the prodigal may be restored to the family. The God who gives up his only Son is the Father not merely running towards but giving himself up to the rough treatment of the very ones who reject his fatherly rule, and for their sake. In this way, the notion of sacrifice, tired and misused as it often is, remains a matchless conceptual expression of the theological significance of all that Jesus began and continued among us.

To conclude the section, we return to the point made earlier by reference to George Caird's remark about human abhorrence for sin considered as pollution. 'It is for this reason that the New Testament so constantly employs the language of sacrifice to declare the benefits of the Cross.' Hence 'the imperative need of those whom sin has defiled is that which can cleanse the conscience from dead works (Heb. 9.14)' (Caird 1980 p.17). Because what is happening is not a transaction outside the human sphere, but is a divine action from within the heart of the human condition, it does signal a real change in the human relationship to God. How it might be conceived to be so is not the main topic here, and will concern us later. But before we move to a more systematic treatment of the matter, there is one final instance of metaphorical development to note. Paul uses sacrificial imagery not only of Christ but also of the Spirit: 'We ourselves, who have the *first-fruits* of the Spirit' (Rom.8.23, cf Brown 1978); like that at the heart of Chapter 4, our metaphor also leads us to the hymn to the Spirit in Romans 8. The mention of the eschatological Spirit in such terms comes significantly in a passage concerned with the redemption of the whole creation, which is to be 'set free from its bondage to decay' (v.21). It is not only the human creation that has been defiled; more important, the self-giving of Jesus is part of 'the purpose which he set forth in Christ... to unite all things in him' (Eph.1.10). Such is the richness of this chapter's central metaphor. We shall move, then, from this chapter's outline of some of the chief usages and their implications to an examination of the systematic consequences with the help of a theologian whom it is not unfair to interpret as having this metaphor of atonement at the heart of his concerns, and who shares something of Irenaeus' breadth of understanding of salvation.

III Edward Irving and the Priestly Self-Offering of Christ

One of the objections often made to traditional theologies of the atonement is to the notion of 'transaction'. It is asked whether some supposed transaction between God and the human race taking place millennia ago can be understood to alter the human condition in the present. The dismissive way in which such questions are sometimes asked often betrays a crude parody of the tradition. After all, the transaction can be understood personally rather than merely commercially or legally, as the words of Phillip Doddridge's hymn demonstrate: 'Tis done, the great transaction's done;/ I am my Lord's, and he is mine.' But it is undoubtedly true that theologies centred on a legal or commercial metaphor can degenerate into what appears to be a kind of mathematical balancing of evils: Jesus bears so much evil as a counterweight, so to speak, to ours. Even in Anselm there is a tendency to fall into the trap of drawing out the mathematical rationality of the atonement and so of giving credibility to the charge (*Cur Deus Homo* I xvi-xvii).

CHRIST THE SACRIFICE: A DEAD METAPHOR?

One of the central aims of Edward Irving's christology was to break the dominance of what he called 'stock-exchange divinity'. He rejects the views of those 'who resolve all divinity into a debtor and creditor account' (Irving 1828 p.506) on one very simple ground: that even if Jesus has borne the sins of all humankind, the applicability of the action to us in the present is by no means implied. '(T)he sinner might turn upon us, and say, That example of the sinfulness of sin, which you educed from Christ, is not applicable to me, who have but my own sin to bear' (Irving 1865 p.218). If, accordingly, we are to be able to conceive that past historical life as bearing upon us in the present, it must take account of our plight as it really is. A mathematical, quantitative theology of sin does not do that. Sin, says Irving, 'is not a thing, nor a creature, but it is the state of a creature, – the second state of a creature, in which it is not subject to the law of God, neither indeed can be' (p.218). That being so, the relationship of the creature to God cannot be restored by a legal and quasi-financial balancing act supposed to have taken place in our past.

In order to be able to say with the tradition 'that he bare our sins in His own body on the tree', Irving accordingly has to find a way of expressing the matter that avoids the objectionable overtones of previous conceptions. He does so by resting the weight of his teaching on what would appear to be a development of the sacrificial metaphor. He also reveals his pedigree as a Calvinist, but one who rejects the form that the Calvinist tradition had taken in recent times. We shall understand his theology if we see it as the development of aspects of Calvin's teaching which had been neglected by the Calvinists. In both the *Institutes* and the *Commentary on Hebrews* Calvin insists on the importance of the full humanity of Jesus(*Inst.*II.13.4, *Ad Heb.*7.26, 8.2, 9.14). In the latter work, he stresses the matter in the course

129

of his discussion of the priestly work of Christ. Not only do we find the characteristic claim that 'the Mediator between God and men should himself be a man' (Calvin 1549/1853 p.177), but two features which recur in the theology of Irving. The first is the prominence given to the action of the Holy Spirit in the priestly work of Christ. Neither human nature in itself nor the death Christ suffered as a man can as such be the means of salvation. It is the 'hidden' (Irving 1865 p.180) and 'efficacious' (Calvin p.204) power of the Spirit which gives significance to this particular sacrificial self-giving. The second stress is on what we may call Jesus' Jewish particularity. '(H)is flesh, which proceeded from the seed of Abraham, since it was the temple of God, possessed a vivifying power; yea, the death of Christ became the life of the world' (p.180). There are in Calvin elements of a substitutionary understanding of the atonement; indeed, it seems unlikely that any conception that remains true to the Bible can avoid it. What makes all the difference is the way in which different theologies conceive the substitution. What we find in Calvin is a theology which sees in the life and death of Christ a human self-giving which is effective in giving life to others. The metaphor of the temple is here significant. The temple was the place where sacrifices were offered to God, as a means of approach to him. Now the ascended Christ is the means of access by virtue of what he achieved in his human priesthood. 'He is... said to have made a way for us *by his body* to ascend into heaven, because *in that body* he consecrated himself to God... (H)e for this reason intercedes for us in heaven, because he had put on our flesh, and consecrated it as a temple to God the Father' (p.202, my italics).

The question to which Irving directed his attention with utter singlemindedness is that arising from the concrete particularity of the flesh of Jesus, 'the seed of Abraham'. In the Western tradition it had become customary to teach that the flesh which the Word took on becoming incarnate was that of unfallen Adam. Indeed, in some parts of Christendom it has come to be taught that Jesus was conceived immaculately, and that the Virgin herself was free of human fault. Irving's denial of such doctrines brought against him a charge of heresy, because it appeared that he taught that Jesus was actually sinful. But we can now understand that he was not a heretic, but in fact taught what is one of the pillars on which the doctrine of the atonement rests. What is it to be born a human being under the conditions in which human births universally take place? It is to share in a network of corruption, in which a disseminated pollution – and we should recall here the concept of sin as uncleanness which forms the background to a discussion of the significance of sacrifice – infects the matter from which human being is formed. There is nothing else. 'That Christ took our fallen nature is most manifest, because there was no other in existence to take' (Irving 1865 pp.115f). It is important to be quite clear what is Irving's conception of sin. As we have already heard, 'It is not a thing, nor a creature, but it is the state of a creature... it is the creature man working against the Creator God' (p.218). In all this Irving rejects a mathematical conception of sin: 'This... is not, as it were, the accumulation of the sins of all the elect; but the simple, single, common power of sin diffused throughout, and present in, the substance of flesh of fallen human nature' (p.217). It would not be far wrong to say that Irving has a relational conception of sin. The point is that because all matter is caught up in the human rebellion against God, it is all infected by a diffused corruption. The inescapable conclusion is that any human being will be constituted of corrupt material.

But that takes us to the point of Irving's conception of salvation also. The flesh which the eternal Word takes is, so to speak, a random but also representative sample of the infected whole. It is the Holy Spirit who is the effective agent of what happened in and with the humanity of Christ and, first of all, in its beginnings: 'The substance of created manhood in an unquickened state He took, as I may say, at random, and formed of it the body of Christ' (p.154). This body, consisting as it does of fallen flesh, is yet kept from sin by the agency of the Spirit, and so becomes the first instance of restored humanity and the basis of redemption for others.

> As unfallen creation stood represented in unfallen Adam, so fallen creation stood represented in Christ; and as in Adam's fall all together fell, so in Christ's resurrection shall all be made alive again. This is the first part of imputation: that He freely came under, without any obligation of whatever kind, the load and burden of a fallen world's infirmity and sin. (p.154)

By 'imputation' Irving does not mean that God is punishing Jesus instead of us or that there takes place some merely theoretical transaction; that is precisely what he is trying to avoid by eschewing a mathematical or merely juridical conception of sin. If, he says, we see the death of Christ as 'merely the bearing of so much inflicted wrath, vengeance and punishment' we lose the need to find in the Spirit the agent of the accomplishment of Christ's work (p.234). It is, moreover, 'degrading' to see the Father as punishing Jesus; that makes 'altogether void the Father's activity in the sufferings and death of Christ' (p.147). Rather, the emphasis must be on the events as a new beginning for humanity deriving from the redemptive way in which this human life was lived, a new beginning willed from eternity by the love of the Father. Some forms of expression – 'the continual and exclusive doctrine of debt and payment, of barter and exchange; of suffering for suffering, of clearing the account' (p.225) – in effect turn the atonement into the mere 'reforming of a mistake' (p.315) and lose the notions of grace and covenant as well as

> high discourse concerning the mystery of His person, as God-man; the beauty of grace, the excellence of that constitution of being which He possessed... The Church likewise, by the profit–and–loss theology, by this divinity of the exchange, hath come to lose the relish of that most noble discourse, which treateth of the grandeur and glory of the risen Christ wielding the sceptre of the heavens, yet, from His peerless height of place, consenting to cast His eye perpetually upon the poorest, the meanest, the most deeply tried and overwhelmed of all His people. (pp.225f)

In all this, Irving has put his finger unerringly on the weakness of Western atonement theology. He is, however, aware that legality is involved (p.188) and that the life and death of Jesus may be described as victory. 'The flesh of Christ was the middle space on which the powers of the world contended with the Holy Spirit dwelling in His soul. His flesh' – because it is the battleground of the fallen creation and the Spirit – 'is the fit medium between the powers of darkness and the powers of light' (p.161). It is, we might say, Aulén without myth, because the battle is centred on the human Christ's engagement in his own body with the powers of evil. But it is the imagery of priesthood and sacrifice which takes centre stage, because by its means it becomes possible to see the atonement in terms of grace, gift and love; and not the atonement only, but the whole economy, everything that happens between God and his world. 'The *humiliation* was the sacrifice; the *becoming* man, the *being made flesh*' (p.270, Irving's italics). The death of Jesus is not then isolated from the whole and made into a substitutionary killing, but – as we found in tracing victory through ministry to cross and resurrection – is understood as the climax of the self-giving and the gift of the life of the incarnate on our behalf: 'the blood, which is the symbol of life... fell upon the earth... that is, He gave a life for us' (p.144). Indeed, the sacrifice is one 'made from the foundation of the world' (p.295). The sufferings of Christ are, on this account, not substitutionary – for 'to have punished one that was innocent with the consequences of sin seems... contrary to the holiness of God' so much as 'vicarious, that is, undergone for others' (pp.28f).

It may appear that Irving, in his anxiety to correct an imbalance from the past, has overreacted, placing too much weight on the life, too little on the death of Jesus as the centre of the atonement. It may be, also, that we cannot entirely dispense with substitution, however carefully we qualify it. Yet this nineteenth century theology is highly instructive in two respects. *Dogmatically*, it brings to the centre stage the active humanity of Jesus as one of the bases of reconciliation, similarly to Anselm, but with less of a dualism between God and man in Christ. *Linguistically*, so to speak, it shows something of the way in which the metaphor of sacrifice enables us to speak theologically about the atonement. We have seen that according to Irving the life, death and resurrection of Jesus are all alike the gift of free, transforming grace. But in what sense is the new beginning, the sinful flesh made perfect by obedience in the Spirit, to be understood as effective for the rest of the still fallen creation? We now move from the sacrifice of Christ to his priesthood. In conformity with the thought of the Letter to the Hebrews, Irving sees the active, human obedience of Jesus to be the heart of the matter. This obedience is, so to speak, transferable because Christ is priest as well as sacrifice. The one who is the gift to us of God the Spirit becomes the one who gives to his people the Spirit who had been the means of his true humanity. The 'change of roles' takes place at the resurrection. It is then that Christ the sacrifice becomes the priest, able to baptise with the Holy Spirit (pp.129f). This is why the risen Christ, the first-born from the dead, is the second Adam 'become a quickening spirit' (p.45, quoting 1 Cor.15.45). Thus Christ's life is the prototype of the Spirit's work and, by virtue of the power of the same Spirit which maintained him in sinless obedience and was the agent of his resurrection, is now the means of being able to 'take up humanity into Himself' (p.148). He who until his death was the gift of the Spirit to the world now becomes the giver, in both cases through the gift and will of the Father.

IV   The Logic of Sacrifice

As we look back over the themes of this chapter, we can realise something of the appropriateness of what Irving has done. First, he has been able to develop a remarkably consistent and original theology which is yet open to enrichment from many streams of biblical witness. There are echoes and more than echoes of many New Testament themes. The Epistle to the Hebrews' powerful presentation of the human self-giving of Jesus is clearly at the heart of the development, as is that letter's stress on the ascension as the place where the human and historical Jesus is, without loss of his humanity, raised to a position of eternal priesthood by virtue of his resurrection. The Synoptic Gospels are also everywhere to be seen making their presence felt, for Irving is able, as few theologians have been, to give due weight to all aspects of the human story and yet to see it also as the action of God. Equally, he is able to call on the Johannine tradition, in developing the Fourth Gospel's teaching that it is by virtue of his return to the Father that Jesus is able to become the channel of the Spirit by whose power his own life had become the perfect offering to the Father (see Irving 1865 p.129). Nor is Paul absent, for the often puzzling aspects of 1 Cor.15.45ff are also brought into the symphony: 'the first man being a living soul, the second a quickening spirit' (p.105). Because the talk is of a metaphorical but real sacrifice, we should not expect all of the biblical expressions to say precisely the same thing, but to contribute at different levels and in different places to our understanding of the many-sided event. Irving's treatise enables us to see the point of many of the New Testament characterisations of the humanity of Jesus and his relation to the Spirit.

The second important contribution made by this account of the atonement is its development of Calvin's theology of the human priesthood of Christ. Both in Calvin's own theology and more particularly in that of his successors, the fact that salvation came from God as a genuinely human event had tended to be lost. As we saw, the Holy Spirit was for Calvin the, so to speak, efficient power of Christ's sacrifice. If we understand the Spirit to be God as he graciously enables human life to be truly human, we are also able to see the atonement as genuinely the work of God the Father, coming indeed from 'outside' as the outworking of the eternal love of God, but taking shape within an autonomous human life (autonomous because given autonomy by the Spirit).

The third feature of the chapter illuminated by Irving's theology is something we have met in earlier chapters, and it is what has been called the cosmic context in which this and the other metaphors have to be understood. Sacrifice has to do with the rightful ordering of life in the world, and that involves us in taking seriously notions of pollution and uncleanness which extend beyond the merely moralistic. Western theology has by and large lost this dimension and shown a repeated tendency to overmoralize its understanding of the atonement. Its vision has become increasingly anthropocentric and individualistic, at the expense of aspects of the tradition which see salvation as being in and with the whole created order. Because Irving sees fallenness not simply in individual or even human terms but as something disseminated throughout the creation, he is able to conceive the fullness of the promise of redemption, seeing salvation as universal in scope:

> Whether you regard the life of any individual, or the life of the race of men, or the life of animals, or the vegetable life of the world, it is all a fruit, a common fruit of redemption, a benefit of the death of Christ, from all eternity purposed, and so far as God is concerned accomplished also. (pp.295f)

Because Jesus, the Word made flesh – and not just 'a human being' as some theologically impoverished translations have it – gave his life, all life takes its being from him. 'Life we hold of the purchase of Christ's sacrifice made from the foundation of the world' (p.295). The metaphor is thus stretched almost to breaking point: a sacrifice from eternity, taking place in time and returning to eternity with Jesus' resurrection and ascension.

That is Irving's particular contribution to the unfolding of the notion, and it is parallel to what we found in the theologies of Forsyth and Barth in the previous chapter. It is one way in which thought about Jesus is made possible through the focus provided by the metaphor of sacrifice. Particularly in the third point taken from Irving we find the reappearance of one theme that has occurred before. Metaphor, as we have repeatedly found, is a means of the interrelating of mind and reality, of person and world. The metaphors of atonement thus allow not only theology in the strict sense – speech about God – but also features of our life in the world to come into view.

What, then, is the particular contribution that the concept of sacrifice, as it is interpreted by Jesus' manner of living and dying, makes to the pattern that is unfolding before our eyes? Victory, as we saw, centres on the life and death as a particular and unique way of fighting the universal battle against evil. God wins, by the human victory of Christ, the means for us to share, after and through him, in the promised eschatological victory. Similarly, the death of Jesus under the law reveals the way in which God puts right the lawlessness of the universe, not punitively but transformatively, by sheer grace. New possibilities for justice are created by the free human choice of Jesus to suffer rather than to resist or avenge evil. Both metaphors are also remarkable for their capacity to construe human life in its broad context in the world as a whole. Our third metaphor works in parallel with them, and so creates a richer tapestry within the dogmatic frame called 'the doctrine of the atonement'. As we saw, the development begins with the recognition of sin and evil as dirt or pollution. Human life, soiled in a soiled universe, is deprived of its proper direction by sin and its consequences. Such recognition is often accompanied by the belief that the giving of life, the greatest gift of the creator, demolishes the barrier that uncleanness erects, and so restores relationship. Here we reach the heart of the mystery of the atonement, for the life that is given is the life of God himself, the incarnate Son dying for the life of the world.

As in the case of the other metaphors, it is clear that all turns on the matter of relationship. We live in an interrelated universe, so that one part of our world is only what it is by virtue of its relation to all other parts. An atomic explosion, for example, affects in different degrees the weather in other parts of the world. To talk of sin is to talk of a way in which the world is affected by a breach in relationships between humankind and our creator. The breach is partly explicable in terms of pollution, just as it is partly explicable in terms of the breaking of law and slavery to evil. It is a conceptual way of understanding our situation in the world. Correlatively, sacrifice is a term which has served to express a number of similar features shared by those human actions designed to restore relations between God and the world. In the New Testament, features of traditional ways of speech are taken up and combined in such a way that the Father's giving of the Son and Jesus' giving of his life constitute the only sacrifice which can wipe away the accumulated filth. Why? Because in Jesus God deals with the heart. The Letter to the Hebrews (8.8-12) argues that a reconstituting of relations has taken place in the life, death, resurrection and ascension of Jesus. The promise of Jer. 31.31-4 is fulfilled: 'I will put my laws into their minds and write them on their hearts.' It is to be noted that this letter puts very high on its agenda the anthropological question: why has the human creation not fulfilled the promise in Psalm 8 of human stewardship of the creation? The answer is that it has: we do see Jesus. Jesus is the one – 'the author and pioneer of our faith' – who creates and inaugurates a renewal of the human relation to God, by washing from our hands the blood which otherwise continues to stain ourselves and all we touch.

We are not concerned at this stage with the *how* of the matter, with the way in which it may be understood that the heart of stone is in such a way replaced by a heart of true flesh and blood. As in Chapters 3 and 4, the intention is to show what kind of meaning the metaphors of atonement can be shown to have. What, then, is the quality of the sacrifice which makes it uniquely what it is? Daniel Hardy has suggested that at the heart of the meaning of sacrifice is the notion of *concentration*. When, then, we tell the story of Jesus we do not narrate simply the tale of a true, Spirit-led human being, touched but unpolluted by the disseminated corruption through which he passes, but of a human offering of life to the Father, concentrated and overflowing. 'This work' wrote Forsyth, 'was the condensed action of his whole personality' (Forsyth 1962 p.10). Such language also helps us to express the totality of the giving, of God the Father to the world and of the Son in response to the Father. Here is the concentrated life of creation, given by God and returned to him, sweeping away by its sheer concentrated grace and goodness all that stands between holy God and sinful people.

It is this sense of the sheer goodness of God's gift of himself in Jesus that motivates some of the early Christian responses to the sacrifice:

> O sweetest exchange! O unfathomable work of God! O blessings beyond all expectation! The sinfulness of many is hidden within the Righteous One, while the righteousness of the One justifies the many that are sinners. (*Letter to Diognetus* 9.5)

Not here some grim balancing of accounts, but rejoicing in a liberation. The Son of God has given himself to be where we are so that we might be where he is, participants in the life of God. And corresponding to that gift is the complete self-giving that is required, but likewise as a free and glad response. 'I appeal to you therefore...to present your bodies as a living sacrifice, holy and acceptable to God' (Rom.12.1).

We shall return to that theme in another context. But we end this chapter by a return to the question contained in its title. A dead metaphor? It is certainly one that continues to be trivialised and sometimes misused, but that may be in large part by virtue of its inexhaustible appeal. It is that inexhaustibility which accounts also for both the sheer difficulty of handling the topic and the fact that it is the very centre of the doctrine of the atonement. Does not its orientation to life, grace and self-giving, to the concentrated love of God poured out for the creature, take us as far as any human language can into the very heart of God? What, then, is potentially an abused and overused metaphor can also become the most living and expressive of all, the heart of the doctrine of the atonement as an expression of the unfathomable power and grace of God.

6

The Atonement and the Triune God

Batter my heart, three–person'd God;
John Donne

I   Relation

The three metaphors of atonement take their meaning, when understood in depth, from relationships. On one level, the most important but by no means the sole, are the relationships we call personal. All the metaphors can be understood as expressing in human language the significance of the life of a man, born, crucified, risen and ascended, as at once coming from God and bearing upon the life of all human-kind. But that is not the only level at which they are to be understood as bearing upon reality, for they also reveal that Jesus interacts with the whole world in which human life is set. When we speak of a victory over the demonic, we speak of an action performed both for the sake of human lives enslaved to a demonised creation and for the sake of the perfection of that creation. When we speak of the justice of God realised in the life and death of Jesus, we are reminded that our action takes form in a universe whose structures are not, despite our attempts to evade the matter, irrelevant to its outcome. When we speak of sacrifice, we speak of an action of God within and as part of a world polluted by human arrogance and cupidity. Human life is always to be treated in the context of its relationships to the whole of creation.

Alongside the concern for the relationship of God to the human and the whole created order, the argument has also been that metaphor, as representative of all our language, is a reality that relates: it relates speaker to world in such a way that the reciprocal openness of mind to world and world to mind comes into view. This is by no means an automatic matter, for language often fails in its attempt to be true to the world. It certainly never succeeds in saying all that we would wish. We are fallible and sinful mortals, and, in any case, the world has its own depth and, so to speak, privacy. We can look, question, probe, experiment, torture, but, nevertheless, may only speak of that which is opened to our minds. The wonder is that so much can be said. There is a rationality in things, which is reflected in the rationality of words. The wonder of theology is that it is by grace enabled to speak of the rationality of the divine action with the help of language which is also used of such disparate albeit important human activities. The particular glory of the doctrine of the atonement is that by metaphor we are able to speak not simply of some immanent rationality, but of the rationality of redemption. The adaptation of language to new realities comes as the world is made anew in Christ.

The time has come to enquire whether a consistent pattern can be discerned in the various relationships which have come to light. What, in general, is entailed for our understanding of God and the world, human and non-human alike? Who is the God who is claimed to relate himself, in the way our metaphors allow us to say, to the world in which we are set? What kind of world is it; what kind of beings are we, its most problematic inhabitants? If what the metaphors suggest is true, the relationship which determines all the others is that between God and everything else. But its historical and concrete centre takes shape in Jesus who is God's victory, justice and sacrifice. We shall, accordingly, begin there and work upwards and outwards into the various relationships involved. The discussion will provide an opportunity to survey in a new light some of the notorious difficulties of the theology of the atonement.

II God: in the Beginning

If we use the word 'career', inadequate though it is, to serve as a summary of all the things that happened with and to Jesus, his birth, life, ministry, suffering, death, resurrection and ascension, in fact all that he did and suffered, it will form the basis of a theological development of the content of our three central metaphors. And the first thing that must be said in summary is that the whole career is to be understood as the victory, the justifying action and the sacrifice of God. That has already been said in the chapters devoted to the particular metaphors. But it has been said chiefly of the career as an event in past history, of something that has happened in time, in our past. In the Christian tradition great things have been claimed for this happening of God in our midst, and they must, despite contemporary scepticism, based as it is on the Enlightenment's alienated view of time, continue to be said. But on their own, they are not enough. The objection with which this chapter is in part designed to deal is that such a conception of the atonement is 'interventionist', that is, that it represents an abrupt breach in the fabric of nature and of history by an otherwise absent (or less present) deity. It appears to suppose, that is to say, that God once made the world and, now that it has shown itself to be in need of redemption, is compelled, so to speak, to interfere in its otherwise consistent course.

Against such an objection it must on the one hand be said that if it is true that the career of Jesus is decisive for the meaning of our life on earth, there is, in one sense of the word, an intervention. This event is once-for-all, unique and unparalleled, for it is the presence of the eternal Son in person to his world. Many theologies in our past and present do, however, suggest more than that, and the criticisms are not always of parodies. It is easy, particularly in our rather moralistic Western tradition, to hold the realms of nature and grace, of creation and redemption, so far apart that the incarnation is made to appear more 'interventionist' than it ought. On the other hand, however, the classic patristic theologies, particularly those of Irenaeus and Athanasius, stress a continuity in the action of God towards and in the world. For Irenaeus the incarnation is at once an initiative of redemption and the bringing to perfection of the creation. In Athanasius the incarnate one is the Word who is the means of God's continuing presence to the world. Therefore the 'intervention' of God for his world is not isolated from the rest of his action, because it is the mediator of creation who comes to ensure that the original purposes of God do not founder in futility.

The heart of the matter, accordingly, is the newness within continuity of the divine action in atonement. God cannot 'intervene' if he is present to the world already in a continuing dynamism of providence; his presence as incarnate is, indeed, once for all, but not, so to speak, out of character. In different ways our metaphors enable us to show how this matter of the particular action of the eternal God may be conceived as the centre of a history stretching from eternity to eternity. If, then, the career of Jesus is God's victory, justifying and sacrifice, what does it reveal in these terms of the ways of God *in general*?

'Was it not thou that didst cut Rahab in pieces, that didst pierce the dragon?' (Isa.51.9). In these words the 'second' Isaiah draws upon the language of Near Eastern creation myth in order to express the lordship of God over the created order. In so far as the myths express a recalcitrance of the creation or any limitations on the action of God, they are banished from Old Testament usage, and their language used only to express the opposite: the utter freedom of God over against the cosmos. Westermann, indeed, denies the once common belief that there is an allusion to mythical language in Gen.1.2 (Westermann 1974/1984 pp.103, 105f). In particular, 'There is no sign at all of any struggle between God and תהום corresponding to the struggle between Marduk and Tiamat' (p.106). This means that we cannot speak of the creation of the world by God as a kind of victory if by that is meant a struggle to overcome some opposing and recalcitrant power. But there is a victory of a kind, over the darkness and chaos against the background of which Genesis shows the creation to take place. In the Bible's characterisation of the very beginning of things we see the metaphor of victory employed to depict the creator's complete authority over that which is made by him. Where other myths had portrayed the world as the product of a battle between gods or as a process of giving birth, Israel came to conceive everything as subservient to the rule of the one God. That is why there is in the Old Testament no final divorce between history and cosmology. Some of the Psalms, for example, speak of he Exodus in such a way that the historic liberation is shared by the cosmos, while Psalm 104.5-9 interweaves the languages of creation and the covenant with Noah. Creation is all of a piece, because of the victorious rule of God over and in it. Leviathan, the great beast, is not now the defeated monster who becomes the world, but simply part of the furniture of the one creation (Ps. 104.26: 'Leviathan which thou didst form to sport in (the sea)'). For our purposes, the point is that the rule of God in creation, his conquest over such evil which afflicts history and the cosmos, is grounded in his 'victory' in the beginning.

If creation is a victory, it is also right to call it, in the broadest sense of the word, a justification.[1] It is the movement by which things, in the beginning, are placed in their due order. In no sense is creation a neutral act for the biblical writers. The affirmation of the work of God 'in the beginning' is well expressed in the refrain of Genesis 1, whose climax is in verse 31: 'And God saw everything that he had made, and, behold, it was very good.' A similar point is made by Psalm 104, whose celebration of the goodness of the creation is achieved by drawing pictures taken both from the history of salvation and from the everyday life of nature. It is not, however, a naïvely optimistic or static rendering, as if no further divine justification were required; and the writer is aware that death, too, is part of the just order: 'when thou takest away their breath, they die and return to their dust' (v.29). To this can be added the witness of the Wisdom literature as a whole, which is misunderstood both if it is interpreted through moralistic eyes as an aberration from the true path of salvation history and if it is treated as primitive natural theology. It belongs, rather, in Israel's tradition of seeing all things as deriving from the gift of the one creator. The expression of creation as justification is therefore grounded in the kind of concept of God to which von Balthasar makes reference: 'In addition to other meanings relating to man's justification and derived from its primary sense, *justitia Dei* above all means the rightness (*Richtigkeit, justesse*) of everything pertaining to God' (Von Balthasar 1967/1982 p.472). The only question to be asked of von Balthasar is whether the use of the concept in human justification is truly the primary sense. Perhaps the latter is the derived sense, and the primary reference is the overall goodness of the way in which God is both in himself and towards what is not God: human

1. See Barth 1945/1958 pp.366ff, where Barth argues that part of the Yes of God to the creation is its justification. 'The reality which it has and is, is not just any reality. Its being is not neutral; it is not bad, but good' (p.366).

justification is but an aspect of the justification of all things by their creator.

Thus our first two metaphors can be shown to throw light on the ways of God towards his creation in general. The purpose of such a development is to build a theological basis for a non-interventionist concept of the atonement which yet maintains the utter uniqueness and definitiveness of the career of Jesus. But the third? When Rev.13.8 (cf 1 Pet.1.20, John 17.24) speaks of 'the lamb slain from the foundation of the world' we should not take it to be fancifully projecting back into the past an event from recent history. If Jesus is the sacrificial self-giving of *God*, we must take it with every seriousness as an insight into the eternal being of the Godhead. The temporal sacrifice which is the 'giving up' (Rom. 8.32, John 3.16) or 'sending' (Rom. 8.3) of the Son is not an act foreign to the deity, not an isolated intervention, because it springs from what God is in eternity. For this reason, it is not a mistake to conceive creation, too as a function of the self-giving of God, in which out of the free, overflowing goodness of his life he gives reality and form to something that is other than himself, simply for its own sake.

In these brief sorties into the doctrine of creation, one point is being made: that to interpret the career of Jesus as the historic victory, justice and sacrifice of God is not to speak of something uncharacteristic, something coming merely 'from outside'. Modern theology finds it difficult not to think deistically, and so tends to see the world either as externally related to God or as a self-sufficient entity, complete and self-enclosed. On such conceptions, the historic atonement appears to be a breach in the seamless cloth of creation. But if we learn, with the help of our metaphors, the Bible and the great theologians of every age, to realise the interrelatedness of redemption and creation, that both are the fruit of the way in which the world is what it is through the free self-relating of God to it, we shall not so easily be led astray. We shall be freed to conceive the redemptive action of God in Jesus as of a piece with his just and sacrificial ordering of all things.

III   God: in the End

If, however, we are to be true to the biblical accounts of creation, other forms of static thinking must also be eschewed. Creation may be very good and even, in its own way, complete, but it is only so if room is made to allow that it is directed to an end. That is particularly important when we are concerned with the doctrine of redemption. Some stress has been placed on the fact that sin, as it is understood as the other side of the atonement, is a form of disorder, disorder affecting both the person and the creation as a whole. On such an account, the atonement is a reordering, a setting right of that which has been disrupted. But if that reordering is understood as merely a restoring to origins, as no more than a restoration, there is a danger that it will be conceived as merely or mainly conservative in form (as, sad to relate, has often been the case). Against such a limitation it must be stressed that redemption is not merely a removal of disorder but a redirection and a liberation: it is a resurrection.

We take up the argument with the rehearsal of a central theme of the previous section, that things are what they are in virtue of the victory, justice and, as self-giving, sacrifice of God in the beginning. We are therefore bound to conclude that God created all things *through* his Son or Word, who *is* his victory, justification and sacrifice. In the apparent aside of 1 Cor. 8.6, Paul speaks of 'one Lord, Jesus Christ, through whom are all things', and similar points are made in John 1.1f and Heb.12f. Yet, without any inconsistency, it is also proclaimed that Christ is the end of creation, that to which it aims: 'to unite all things in him, things in heaven and things on earth' (Eph.1.10, cf the 'for him' of Col.1.16). The past ordering, which is the victory of the just God over chaos, is not the making of a static and perfect whole, a deist machine, but the setting in motion of that which has a destiny in the freedom of the Spirit.

If the uniting of all things in Christ is purposed from the beginning, certain consequences follow. The first is that the basis of the atonement is what has been termed 'prelapsarian'. It is the purpose of God from eternity to bring his creation to perfection through his relation to it through his Son, independently of whether or not sin supervened. Here we meet a difficulty. All the metaphors which have been the vehicles of the development so far appear to take their shape not from such a completion of the creation, but from the active overcoming of evil which is the meaning of Jesus' career. That would appear to imply that the cause of what happened with Jesus was not the love of God from eternity, but the *failure* of the original purpose; or that there is no continuity between creation and atonement, because the incarnation appears to be an entirely different matter from creation. In either case, the continuity in the meaning of our metaphors is in danger of being lost.

What is the status of the sin and evil over which God in Christ triumphed? Irving argued that sin is the 'immediate' and 'also the formal cause of the incarnation; that is to say, what gave to the purpose of God its outward form and character' (Irving 1865 p.10). In other words, the incarnation took the form it did – leading to a judicial execution and ritual sacrifice – because the end of creation, given the way things had turned out, could be achieved only by one able so to enter the network of slavery, evil and corruption as to free the good creation from its meshes. Sin and evil on such an understanding are those corruptions which impede the creation's achievement of its promised perfection.

The second implication of the teaching that all things are to be reconciled in Christ is that the metaphors must be understood from the end as well as from the beginning, as has already been suggested in the chapters devoted to them. Indeed, it may be said that in the light of the resurrection of Jesus they should be understood primarily in that way. Such is undoubtedly the case with the concept of victory. As a victory, the cross is final in the sense that it is the decisive meeting, in the midst of fallen time, of the person of the Word incarnate and the powers holding the creation in thrall. It is as such the signal, pledge and first fruits of the final victory when God shall be all in all. God reigns now through Christ, and in anticipation of the 'time' when that victory shall be complete. That, without doubt, is at least part of the point made by the puzzling vv.20–22 of Paul's extended discussion of the resurrection in 1 Corinthians 15. They imply that victory is achieved only where Christ, risen and so the first fruits of victory, exercises his rule. 'Then comes the end, when he delivers the kingdom to God the Father after destroying every rule and authority and power.' The Son is the agent of the Father's victory in the world, but when all is complete the economy – the historic presence of the triune God to the world in creation and redemption – will likewise be complete.

It is, in this context, to be noted that according to the passage from Paul 'the last enemy to be destroyed is death' (v.26). We recall the words of Psalm 104.29, which appear to imply that death is part of the good order of the creation, and so can appreciate another facet of the distinction in continuity between the orders of creation and redemption. In the conditions of fallenness, death is no longer part of the good order of things, but meets us as judgement, destruction and defeat. It has been conquered by the saving resurrection of Jesus, but also has continually to be overcome in fact and as promise by the action of the creator Spirit. So it is that Paul can see evil and suffering, the ministers of death, as realities whose power is broken, but which have to be endured in hope (Rom.5.3ff). That, also, is one of the chief themes of the Apocalypse, which depicts the suffering of the persecuted church both as resulting from the victory of the lamb and to be endured in hope until the final victory, when the sea, symbol of evil and death, will be no more (Rev. 21.1).

The other metaphors, similarly though not so obviously, give up their full meaning only eschatologically. Even if, with Forsyth, we conceive the justice of God as taking shape in the regeneration of the wicked, it is finally a concept which is filled out only from the end. That is why it is a mistake to picture human destiny in terms of a return to paradise. The Western tradition in particular has tended to fit the human story into the schema of a beginning in paradise, a fall into disgrace and a restoration to former glory. The concept of the justice of God makes better sense in a more Irenaean form, in terms, that is, of God's bringing to completion that which was begun with the creation. Here, despite the tendency of much modern theology to be over–influenced by the notion of evolution, there is no doubt that the concept of development is a useful one. So long as it is not supposed that evolution is an automatic process, or one which operates purely immanently, so that human destiny is built into the fabric of things, it is helpful in showing that nothing is complete in the beginning. Justification means that God in his freedom as Spirit will bring to perfection that which was begun, despite the worst efforts of the creation to resist. It means the completion of the creation, in spite of and beyond our 'injustice', not by compulsion but by means of the transformation of human possibilities in Christ.

Combining the metaphors, we can say that the sacrifice which the victorious and risen Son makes to the Father *is* the perfected creation. Hence, Colossians speaks (1.22) of the end of the reconciling death of Christ to be 'to present you holy and blameless and irreproachable before him': as, we might gloss, a perfect sacrifice. Moreover, according to the Letter to the Hebrews, it is as sacrifice that Christ is judge, the one who exercises the judgement of God. And what is the outcome of that judgement? 'Christ, having been offered once to bear the sins of many, will appear a second time... to save those who are eagerly waiting for him' (9.28). The end of all things inevitably involves judgement, the sifting of the good from the bad, just as it involves the final victory over evil. But the process is not, as traditional imagery of heaven and hell sometimes suggests, oriented equally to heaven on the one side and hell on the other. There is indeed a judgement, but it is an eschatology of promise through judgement, not of promise and threat in equal balance (see here 1 Cor. 3.12-15). Victory, justification and sacrifice alike are oriented to the end, and they conceive the atonement in terms of the perfection of the creation, in the Son's bringing to the Father a renewed and completed world.

In such ways as these, then, the metaphors enable us to express something of the work of the triune God through, in and with his creation. The purpose of the Father achieved by the incarnation, cross and resurrection of the incarnate Son has its basis in the creation by which the world took shape, and will find its completion in the work of the Spirit who brings the Son's work to perfection. We can speak in this way because the metaphors enable us to conceive the career of Jesus as the victory, sacrifice and justice *of God*, and so to write that particular story into a determinative place in the narrative of the ways of God with the world. But to say that is only to begin to spell out its theological consequences.

IV Subjective and Objective

In the previous sections there were drawn out some of the implications of saying that the human career of Jesus is also the decisive action of God in and towards his world, and is therefore both the centre point of, and clue to, the way in which God is related to the world from beginning to end. When we turn to the human dimensions, we have to ask about the way in which that same career is not simply the victory, justification and sacrifice of a man but at the same time takes up into itself and realises the life of the creation. In asking such a question, we come first of all face to face with a matter which has often been near the surface of the discussion, and has dominated the history of the doctrine of the atonement, certainly in the West. (One of the reasons for the way this book has been structured is a hope that the aridities of some previous debates could be avoided.) In relation to the rest of us, is Jesus a substitute, a representative, an example, or some combination of them all? At the outset, two preliminary points must be made. The first is that to ask the question in that way is misleading, because it may suggest that the three notions are fixed in meaning and clearly understandable simply as concepts. There lies the danger of abstraction, of bringing to the topic assumptions which obscure. If all or any of the three are to be found to be appropriate, it will be because they enable us to give some account of the meaning of Jesus, and so have their meaning controlled by him.

The second preliminary point is that the underlying systematic question, that of the universal or inclusive meaning of Jesus, meets us in a particular form at our place in the theological history of Western Christianity. We saw in Chapter 1 how three seminal thinkers in our tradition made particular rational criticisms of the traditional way in which the atonement had been taught. Some years before them, Socinian theologians had voiced specific attacks on the notion of substitution. As Harnack shows in his account of Socinianism (Harnack 1885/1899 pp.118-167), the movement's objection to substitutionary theologies of the atonement combined what he calls Scotist doctrines of God with Pelagian tendencies in anthropology. By Scotist doctrines of God he means in effect appeals to omnipotence: God, if he wants, is entirely free to remit sin without penalty. Why, then, is there any need for Jesus to suffer in our place?[2] The Pelagian arguments appeal to notions of the untransferability of guilt: guilt is individual and particular, and cannot therefore be taken by or transferred to another. They are Pelagian in the sense that an underlying assumption of the arguments is that actions cannot be determined, given or enabled by another, even if that other be God, but must be produced by the individual alone. The Enlightenment, especially with Kant's development of a strong if nuanced notion of individual autonomy, strengthened the tendency to Pelagianism, with the result that God came to be conceived as a competitor of, or threat to, human freedom rather than its source.

The allusion to the Pelagian tendencies of the Enlightenment has been repeated here because it shows why 'subjective' or 'exemplarist' forms of the theology of the atonement have become increasingly popular in recent times. The terms *subjective* and *exemplarist* refer to different aspects of a single approach to the topic. The former calls attention to

2. Appeals to omnipotence are almost always unsatisfactory, being in effect abstract appeals to logical possibility rather than arguments from the way in which God is in his action. In this particular case, they are undermined by the shape the concept of the justice of God takes in the light of the considerations advanced in Chapter 4 above.

the contention that the central feature of a doctrine of the atonement is the effect the life and/or death of Christ should have upon the believer. What matters, it is argued, is that there should be repentance, a new moral seriousness, Christian love and the like. Exemplarism, on the other hand, stresses the objective basis of the doctrine, holding the love of God and the life of Jesus to be examples the believer must follow rather than a substitutionary transaction – as the opposing view is often parodied – changing the human status before God. (Clearly, there is no need for substitution in the light of the 'Scotist' belief that God can do exactly what he likes.)

We shall return to the matter of substitution. Our present concern, however, is with the adequacy of an exemplarist doctrine of the atonement. And first it must be accepted that both God and Jesus are used in the Bible as examples for human imitation. Israel's calling is to be holy as God is holy (Lev.11.44, cf Matt.5.48), or, more generally, to reflect in her life's orientation the pattern of God's goodness in choosing them to be his people. Similarly, the Synoptic Gospels present the cross as something to be 'taken up' in imitation of Jesus' example. For Paul, the notion of following an example appears frequently, but it is worth referring, once again, to Rom.12.1, where the recipients of the letter are told to 'present your bodies as a living sacrifice', in clear echo of the sacrifice of Jesus. Similarly in the Johannine tradition, in another passage we have met before, faith is seen as victory which overcomes the world. If, therefore, we are to establish a case for an objective, past atonement, it cannot be at the cost of denying the subjective and exemplary implications. The story of Jesus, whatever else it tells, is presented as an example, a supreme pattern to follow (Heb.12.2), the one example of a genuine human life in the midst of a fallen world.

The reference to the Letter to the Hebrews, however, introduces the reasons why a merely subjective or exemplarist theology is inadequate. The first is that it takes passages from the Bible out of context and makes what is a part, and a part consequent on the priority of divine initiative, into almost the whole. Without prefacing, for example, the exhortations to follow Jesus with a theological account, expounding his saving significance on the basis of which imitation is *reasonable* (Rom. 12.1 again), the imitation hangs in the air. That consideration brings us to the second, dogmatic reason for the inadequacy of a purely or largely exemplarist doctrine. Jesus is an example because he and he alone is the incarnate Son who by the enabling of the Holy Spirit remained unfallen where we universally fall. His humanity is only what it is because it is that of the one sent by the Father through the Spirit. As the only human victory, the life of the one just man, the only true offering of free obedience to the Father, *this particular* humanity is what it is because it is his who is sent by the Father to save lost mankind. There is no treatment of the person of Christ in the New Testament which does not place it in the context of its end in the redemption of the creation, the reconciliation of all things in Christ.

Furthermore, – and this brings us to the third reason for the inadequacy of a mainly exemplarist treatment of the atonement – there is no treatment which does not also make the death and resurrection of Jesus the pivot of the events in which the reconciling action takes place. The fact that the ministry and mission of Jesus led to his death dominates the narrative in all its forms, gospel and epistle alike, so completely that no treatment of the Christian theology of salvation which wishes to be true to scripture is possible apart from it. We have seen that the death and the way Jesus approached it is indeed set before the New Testament's readers as an example (and see here especially Phil. 2.5ff). But what, to use a hackneyed illustration, distinguishes this death from that of Socrates? The latter's death is often presented as the paradigm of the true philosopher's welcoming of death as the casting off of the shackles of the flesh in order to return to timeless eternity (Plato, *Phaedo*). For Christian theology, by contrast, the death of Jesus has generally been represented as having to do first with the perfection and completeness of his life as human (so Heb. 5.8: 'he learned obedience through what he suffered'); and second with its determination as an act of God (hence the appeal of Isa.53.10: 'it was the will of the Lord to bruise him'). That is not to say *tout court* that God punishes Jesus instead of us but that the death of Jesus is first of all to be understood as part of the divine purpose of redemption. In the language of sacrifice, God 'gives up', hands over his Son to death. Why?

In his 'Subjective and Objective Conceptions of Atonement' (MacKinnon 1966), Donald MacKinnon argues that the crucial weakness of subjective theologies of the atonement is that they trivialise evil. Anselm has a similar point with his 'Have you not considered how great is the weight of sin?'(*Cur Deus Homo* I,xxi). Although Anselm's may, as has been remarked already, appear to be a rather quantitative way of putting the matter, it draws attention to the fact that the human condition is too enmeshed in evil to be able to be restored by its own agency. Forgiveness is not, therefore, simply a matter of omnipotence: something God can do simply because he wants to. A mere declaration changes nothing. It is the proponents of subjective theories who are, for this reason, in danger of succumbing to an atonement of legal fiction, as they often accuse their opponents of doing. The point could be reinforced by a discussion of the concept of sin which is implied in any of the three metaphors of atonement, although it is done most easily by a reference to the discussion of the demonic. On such an account, sin is a slavery, and slavery is not abolished by appeals to follow a good example. What is required is a setting free, an act of recreation, of redemption, which yet respects the humanity of its object.

All three of our metaphors operate with a double focus, on both God and the world. They reveal that the problem which the atonement engages is primarily *theological*. It does not consist primarily in morally wrong acts whose effect is on human life alone and which can therefore be rectified by merely human remedial action, but in a disrupted relationship with the creator. As a result of the disruption there is an *objective* bondage, pollution and disorder in personal and social life, encompassing all dimensions of human existence and its context. By virtue of both truths, that the problem is one we cannot solve and that our being clean and free and upright is the gift of the creator, there needs be a recreative, redemptive divine initiative in which the root of the problem, the disrupted personal relationship, is set to rights.

V   Representation and Substitution
The three metaphors, accordingly, form the basis and framework of an account of the divine initiative, in that they enable us to think systematically about the recreating action of God, without ever supposing that we have plumbed its depths in an exhaustive rational account. The victory theme tells that there is something intractable and demonic, the accumulated enslaving weight of idolatry and falsehood to be overcome. It shows that the liberation is achieved where the slavery was entered, on the field of human moral struggle. There is, however, no suggestion of recreation by fiat, by the mere exercise of omnipotence, because the means of victory is the humble Son of God's recapitulation of the human progress from birth, through death and beyond, in a

conquest of the power of the demonic by faithfulness and truth. It is a victory that only God can win, but he wins it from within human reality, engaging personally with the radical depersonalisation of the world.

Similarly, the metaphor of justice derives, as we have seen, from a broader conception of human life in the world than the merely legal or forensic. But it demonstrates that there can be no restoration of relationships unless the nature of the offence against universal justice is laid bare and attacked as its root. P.T. Forsyth's assault on those theologies which would trivialise the grossness of human evil was buttressed by an insistence on the *holy* love of God. Holiness is of purer eyes than to behold human iniquity; but it does. As man, the eternal Son of God, God's outgoing love, allows the consequences of human evil to fall upon his head. Evil is thus taken seriously: as seriously as it can be, for its destructive consequences are accepted and borne. Correspondingly, the metaphor of sacrifice calls attention to the manner in which the the divine action in the world is effected: by the Father's sending of the Son who, by virtue of the Spirit's humanising action, returns the first fruits of a true, recapitulated human life to the Father. By entering the sphere of our pollution, by touching tar and yet not being defiled, humanity pure and undefiled is brought to the Father as a concentrated offering of worship and praise.

There is too much in all this to be accounted for solely or mainly in terms of an example, example though it is. Jesus is indeed man before God, but only as he is also God among men in his conquering and holy love. The chains must first be broken, the pollution cleansed. The logic is inescapable: if Jesus is man before God, then he must be said either to *represent* or to be a *substitute* for the rest of us. It is sometimes suggested that the former is a preferable alternative to latter, in that it avoids the objectionable notion that Jesus is, as a man, punished by God in our stead. *Representation* is certainly a very useful concept, as we shall see, but much hangs on what is made of it. If, with Sölle (1965/1967), we understand Jesus as a temporary representative, one who stands in for us until we can, so to speak, stand upon our own feet, the outcome is again Pelagian and exemplarist. We do not really require Jesus for our salvation here and now. But there are other less immediately objectionable conceptions of representation, like that of Moberly (1901).[3] He suggests that the penal aspects of the passion of Jesus be taken as a kind of representative penitence. Jesus is not punished in our place, but accepts on our behalf the requirement to repent before God. Moberly is here not far from the Kingdom, for he emphasises the fact that because Jesus' humanity is the humanity of deity, it stands 'in the wide, inclusive consummating relation... to the humanity of all other men' (p.90). What, then, he asks, does 2 Cor. 5.21 mean when it says that Christ was 'made sin' for us? Moberly rightly opposes the dualistic idea, so deeply ingrained in the minds of both its supporters and opponents in the main Western tradition, that Jesus as man is punished by God in place of others. But he also accepts that the human person is affected by an objective weight of transgression and guilt whose removal is the precondition of true obedience. 'There must be something in the direction of undoing of the past, without which indeed the present obedience would not be in its true sense really possible' (p.116). Because, then, a perfect obedience is not sufficient to achieve all that is required, Moberly argues that Jesus offers before God a vicarious penitence. 'In respect of this

3. One of Moberly's aims was to adapt and defend part of the thesis of J.McL. Campbell (1864), who appears to share Moberly's fatal weakness, a final collapse into exemplarism (see Paul 1961 p.167).

guilt of sin, consummated and inhering, human nature could only be purified by all that is involved in the impossible demand of a perfect penitence' (p.117). The one who does not need to be penitent takes upon himself the burden of sharing our consciousness of sin. He therefore exercises the penitence which, precisely because of our sin, we are unable to do. Moberly asks: 'Is not consummation of penitence, that penitence whose consummation sin makes impossible, the real, though impossible, atonement for sin?' (p.129).

The answer to such a question can only be in the negative, despite the moments of truth in Moberly's account. It is undoubtedly true that the gospel story does depict Jesus as identifying himself with sinful Israel in penitence, as the story of his baptism by John indicates. But the reference to baptism indicates also the deficiencies of such an account. The first is that to be baptised along with penitent Israel is not simply to be penitent, but to place oneself under the judgement of God which John, the prophet, exercises. We cannot write out of the story the justice – judgement – of God which Jesus voluntarily undergoes: the cross is the baptism – death by water – and the cup of God's wrath (Mark 10.38; cf Ps.75.7f, Isa.51.17). In view of what, as a matter of objective fact, has happened, there must be a correspondingly objective demonstration of justice, or the world is a morally indifferent place. The second point follows, that vicarious penitence does not require death on the cross, which is the centre of the gospel accounts and not an unfortunate completion of the human story, as tends to be the case with exemplarist theologies. The outcome of Moberly's account is a – admittedly somewhat beefed up – version of Schleiermacher's view that redemption consists in the transmission of Jesus' God-consciousness to later believers. It is an account in which the transformative and agonistic elements of the cross are lost. Something real had to be undergone.

The third weakness of Moberly's account is that its conception of sin is heavily psychological, centred chiefly upon the rather pietistic concern of the removal of a burden of sinful feelings from the individual. That is, indeed, important, but it is only a part of the deeper disorder which has been illuminated by our exploration of the metaphors. The matter of sin and its removal concerns two realms of being which are not satisfactorily treated in an account which places the weight on vicarious penitence. The first is that acknowledged by Moberly, and it is the question of the undoing of the evil past. The unredeemed past is more than sins and feelings of guilt; it is the objective disruption of the life and fabric of the universe. What is at stake is the movement of all things from their good creation to their destiny in Christ. All the ways of expressing the meaning of the atonement which we have explored unfold the cosmic context of redemption. In such a theatre of war, vicarious or representative penitence is ontologically and conceptually puny. The second realm of being which receives only jejune treatment in Moberly's personalistic account is the matter of relationships. We return to the death of Jesus. That the network of relationships in which he was involved *necessitated* a death and not a good moral example alone is indicative of the fact that we are here concerned with a breach of relationships so serious that only God can refashion them. The metaphors of a universe out of joint, of an indelible stain, are ways of speaking of a world whose relationship to its creator is disrupted to such an extent that only the crucifixion of the incarnate Son is adequate to heal it.

It is in such a context that there is required a concept of substitution, albeit one controlled not by the necessity of punishment so much as by the gracious initiative of God in re-creation. To conceive Jesus as primarily the victim of divine punitive justice is to commit three sins: to treat one metaphor of atonement, the legal, in isolation from the others; to read that metaphor literally and merely personalistically; and to create a dualism between the action of God and that of Jesus. Yet to ignore the fact that Jesus is shown in scripture as bearing the consequences, according to the will of God, of our breaches of universal justice – to forget that he was bruised for our iniquities – is, again, to trivialise evil and to deny the need for an atonement, a restoration of relationships which pays due attention to the way things are with the world. At issue is the actuality of atonement: whether the real evil of the real world is faced and healed *ontologically* in the life, death and resurrection of Jesus.

To put it another way, we have to say that Jesus is our substitute because he does for us what we cannot do for ourselves. That includes undergoing the judgement of God, because were we to undergo it without him, it would mean our destruction. Therefore the 'for us' of the cross and resurrection must *include*, though it is not exhausted by, an 'instead of'. He fights and conquers where we are only defeated, and would continue to be without him; he lives a just life, where we disrupt the order and beauty of the universe, and where without him we should continue to do so; he is holy, as God is holy, where we are stained, and would continue to be but for him. And just because of all this he bears the consequences of the world's slavery and pollution; and he does it because as the Son he accepts the burden as his obedience to the Father.

Here we reach the heart of the offence against autonomy which was seen above (Chapter 1, Section II) to be the chief reason for the modern revolt against the theology of the atonement. To speak of *substitution* carries with it the assumption that to be truly – autonomously – human is to have our being formed not by ourselves but by God. Moreover the centre of the doctrine of the atonement is that Christ is not only our substitute – 'instead of' – but that by the substitution he frees us to be ourselves. Substitution is *grace*. He goes, as man, where we cannot go, under the judgement, and so comes perfected into the presence of God. But it is grace because he does so as God and as our representative, so that he enables us to go there after him. That is what is meant by the ancient teaching that Christ is our mediator. He brings us to the Father as one of us, but does so as one who, because he is God incarnate, is able to do so.

It is for such reasons that substitution and representation are correlative, not opposed concepts. Because Jesus is our substitute, it is also right to call him our representative. The two concepts take their meaning from different aspects of the many sided personal interaction with which we are concerned. In the network of relationships which is the world in interaction with its creator, there are many salient features which can be expressed in language. We need both substitution and representation to begin to do justice to the implications of the decisive events with which we are concerned. In this context, it is also important to remember that we cannot simply read off the theological meaning of such terms like representation from some supposed paradigmatic use, as in representative democracy or the like. Just as the notion of substitution derives largely from metaphors of legality, and must be understood in the context of the justice of God as transformative rather than punitive, so that of representation takes its heart from the world of sacrifice. When the Letter to the Hebrews speaks of Jesus as the author and pioneer of our faith, it is saying that he represents us as man before God in order that we too may participate in a like relationship. Thus representation and substitution are two sides of the one relationship, with Jesus taking our place before God so that we ourselves may come, reconciled, before God.

VI Two Systematic Questions

Two important questions are raised by an argument of the kind that we have been pursuing. The first arises from the claim that substitution and representation are a matter of grace: of the mediator's placing himself where we are so that we may be where he is. In what sense, then, does it follow that God in such a way causes us to be what and who we are? The question arises because to say that Jesus is our substitute (albeit as also our representative) is to say that through him God re-establishes our life in its orientation to its promised perfection. The directedness of our life is now determined not by slavery, lawlessness and pollution, but by grace: by the pull of the Spirit to completion rather than the pull of sin to dissolution. The pressure of the argument is leading to a conclusion that we are not faced with a choice between autonomy and heteronomy, between self-directedness and directedness by another, but between an enslaving or a gracious boundness (as Paul says, between being slaves to sin or slaves to God, Rom. 6.15ff). Here we must be wary of all dualistic and deistic thinking which conceives God's relation to the world logically or causally. Grace is a personal–relational concept, not a substantial or causal one, so that a sharp distinction must be made between grace and mechanical determination. If the matter is put in terms of the action of God the Spirit, the point can be made concretely. Jesus was free in the midst of the pressures towards enslavement to the demonic because his life was maintained in freedom by the action of the liberating Spirit. So it is in general: the Spirit is God enabling the world to be itself, to realise its eschatological perfection. That is a kind of constraint, but the constraint of love, as Paul knew (2 Cor. 5.14).

The second systematic question is related to the first, in that it concerns the matters of constraint and freedom in a different dimension. In what sense may it be claimed that Jesus and his salvation are of universal significance? The question divides into two. Why, it should first be asked, is Jesus claimed not only to have lived victoriously, and the rest, but to have won a victory of universal significance, the promise and guarantee of the final reconciliation of all things to God? The second question is the other side of the first. What prevents the claim of universality from being mere empty rhetoric, unrelated to the way things actually are with the world? If the achievement is universal, where is the evidence? (That, of course, carries within itself the question of the kind of evidence we expect in such an enquiry.) If a satisfactory – which does not mean a final – answer is to be found for the first question, a dualist or deist conception of the relation between the world and God must again be avoided. Such a – deist – conception would assume that God and the world were essentially unrelated beings or realms of being. The world would have its own autonomous being and go its own way, except that God would intervene from time to time, and especially in Jesus' to initiate a change of direction. By contrast, a trinitarian conception enables us to understand the matter relationally.

It has been argued above that the metaphors of atonement encourage us to think in terms of the continuity of creation and redemption. An adequate christology will in such a context first of all direct attention to the fact that as the incarnate Son, Jesus is the one through whom the Father created and upholds all things. It is significant that many of the theologies of salvation in the New Testament, the Pauline (Col.1.13ff), the Johannine (John 1.1ff) and that of the Letter to the Hebrews (1.1ff) all bracket their accounts of salvation in Jesus within a proclamation of his cosmic significance. It follows that the soteriologies presuppose that all creation is from the beginning and at all times in relation with God through the divine Word. Christ is the mediator of salvation because he is also the mediator of creation. The universality of the significance of the cross is therefore based in the universality of the activity of the Word, reaffirmed and realised by the Spirit in the resurrection of Jesus from the tomb.

One of the ways in which the universality of Jesus has been expressed in the dogmatic tradition is by means of the doctrine of the *enhypostasia*, which teaches that the humanity of Jesus takes its particular character from the fact that it is the humanity of the eternal Word. Because it is the Word's humanity, it is real and particular humanity, and yet carries with it significance for the rest of humankind. If the mediator of creation takes flesh, then Jesus is related, as a matter of fact, to all flesh, and, indeed, to the whole order of creation. The claim must be understood dynamically, and in terms of relations: 'the... Word of God comes to our realm, howbeit he was not far from us before. For no part of creation is left void of him' (Athanasius, *De Inc.* 8). The Word therefore comes in person to renew the face of the earth. Underlying such a conception of the relation to the world is the trinitarian bedrock: *to be part of the creation means to be related to the Father through the Son and in the Spirit*. But the creation, and particularly the human creation, has lived as if this relation were not real, and so has become subject to the slavery to sin and corruption. The fact that the Son takes flesh in the midst of time means that the relationship is reordered and renewed: redirected to its original and eschatological destiny.

But – and this brings us to the second side of the question of universality – the reordered relationship has to be realised, to take concrete form in time and space. The *ontological* relationship of creator and created, grounded in the Word and reordered in the enhypostatic humanity of Jesus, must become *ontic*. Christology universalises: but the universal salvation must then take concrete shape in particular parts of the creation. We are accordingly concerned not with myth, with the mere repetition of an event imprisoned in the past, but with a process of recreation which respects the createdness and freedom of that which is reshaped. It is the function of God the Spirit, the Lord and giver of life, to *particularise* the universal redemption in anticipation of the eschatological redemption. All the metaphors we have considered are in some way or other concerned with the creation of space in which the creation has room to breathe and expand, to move in freedom to its appointed end. They are specifications of the way in which the universal atoning work becomes real.

Is all this an evasion, a mere abstraction? It would be, but for the fact that there is a concrete place, a community whose sole purpose is the creation of a form of life in which the victory, sacrifice and justice are to be realised. Scholars have sometimes argued that Col.1.18a, 'He is the head of the body, the church' is an intrusion into a hymn celebrating the cosmic significance of the person and work of Christ. But as its stands, its logic – its *theo*-logic – is impeccable. All the talk of the cosmic Christ, of his work in creation and redemption, must be realised in a community whose life takes place in time and space. The church is called to be that midpoint, the realisation in time of the universal redemption and the place where the reconciliation of all things is from time to time anticipated. Notice that it is not being claimed that there is no salvation outside the church, that those outside the actual institution are lost for ever. It has frequently been claimed, for example by Anselm, that the salvation won by Christ is of such moment as to serve for those who are outside the temporal and spatial limits of the institution, and nothing prevents us from seeking and finding the work of the Spirit in other forms of life than the self-consciously Christian. The point about the Christian community is that it is in receipt of a particular call and mission: to orient itself to the place where the universal salvation of God takes place in time and to embody in community and for the world the forms of life which correspond to it. How this may be conceived to take place will be the theme of another chapter.

7

The Community of Reconciliation

Son of man, can these bones live?
Ezekiel 37.3

I Perplexity

We come now to the climax of the argument, and to its most difficult phase. Let us suppose that the argument of Chapter 2, that metaphor is a vehicle of knowledge; of Chapters 3 to 5, that three traditional Christian concepts can be shown to be meaningful; and of Chapter 6, that the whole process can be shown to be dogmatically legitimate, have been established. Where do we stand? There remain a number of deep and swift-flowing rivers to cross, all of them deriving from a single source. The source is the inescapability of the fact that language takes shape, remains alive, in a community of speech. Which, then, is the community in which the metaphors have taken shape and maintained their currency? There are two candidates. The first is Western culture as a whole, for much of whose history the Christian story has served as a framework. It scarcely requires argument to show that it so operates no longer, except in the kind of survivals we have met from time to time: the debased currency of sacrifice, for example. It is an exaggeration to say, as some do, that religious terms are meaningless in our time. Words like *redemption, grace* and other metaphors of the Christian life abound. It is rather that such words no longer operate at the level of awareness and life which ties them to the theology of the atonement attempted in Chapter 6. Indeed, it may even be possible to suggest that there is a sense in which users of the language are inoculated by the currency of dead and debased metaphors against appropriation of their meaning. In that way, the living tradition of atonement theology is in danger of withering away.

The second possible community of speech is the church. That it is not an entirely separate community is manifest. Members of the church, certainly in the West, are also participants in the culture that historically owes so much to Christianity, but has for the most part left it behind. There is, in any case, much overlap between communities, as we can see with the help of an example taken from another field of discourse. The language of field theory and atomic physics is primarily that of a fairly restricted scientific community, but also shared at a more superficial level by the educated public. So here, the Christian language remains a factor in spoken and written English in general. But the church is the place where the language was shaped and continues to be used. It is here that our deepest river confronts us, for it is widely believed that the metaphors have lost currency in the very place where they have both shaped a tradition and been shaped by it. It would appear that even Christians, perhaps Christians especially, do not know what to do with the language they have received. Nor is it simply a matter of intellectual reception. Perhaps more significant still is the fact of an empirical community which does not appear to live as if some of the claims explored in the previous argument are true. If, for example, Jesus is truly victorious over the powers of darkness, should we really expect to find the kind of community that we do?

A first response to that question would be a reference to the letters of Paul to Corinth, if only as a reminder that the empirical church has always had its troubles. We should not be bewitched by some of the events recorded in the Acts of the Apostles into believing in some golden age in which the whole community was a model of (moderately) enthusiastic discipleship. We are finite beings, on the way to salvation, moving between the resurrection of Jesus and the completion of our pilgrimages. There is, to be sure, a sense in which Jesus is the climax of a definitive and final victory. Our place really is taken, so that we stand in a new relation to God. But it does not follow, as we have seen, that there is a magical transformation. The past is not so much wiped out as made into the basis on which a transformed style of living may take shape. The church is the place given by God to be the living space of this new formation, but there can be no suggestion that the inherited weight of evil simply disappears. Because it remains to bedevil the present, it has repeatedly to be laid aside. The church is therefore, it can be argued, no more inherently immune from failure than any other human institution or society.

And yet such a defence is inadequate to meet the case of contemporary conditions. If we are to understand where we are now, a second response must also be sketched. In it two chief points will be made. The first is that the contemporary church is what it is in large measure as a result of the shape it took in the early centuries of our era. It is now battered by inherited ills which it is not yet able to transcend. It was inevitable that, as it grew larger, the early church would come to some understanding of its relationship with the society in which it was taking shape. Unfortunately, it made some wrong choices, and came in effect to provide the ideology which undergirded Western civilisation. To operate as ideology, however, is to provide legitimation for a particular social system, the effect of which may be to prevent the church from living according to the gospel. The result was a contradiction at the very heart of Christendom. The church – though it has never lacked voices urging otherwise – has acquiesced in crusade and inquisition which deny the values for which Jesus died: fighting the battles of God in the way his mode of victory forbids. The point of introducing this well-worn material is not to lay blame so much as to provide some account of why we today find it so difficult to appropriate the language of our tradition. It became diluted because it was taught but in practice denied. We still live in the aftermath of that historical disaster, as in a land polluted long ago by some nuclear accident.

The second point follows from the first. If the settlement which created Christendom introduced contradictions, we have the Enlightenment to thank for their revelation. Modernism is the ideology which lives from the exposure of those contradictions. Its tragedy, and ours, is that it lives from little else: indeed, its contradictions are deeper and more deadly than those of Christendom, largely because of its demonic human self-confidence and lack of a doctrine of sin. But, again, modern Christianity has still to come to terms with its new situation. We are so battered by the winds of doctrine that our chief response to the crisis is often merely to change sides: to side with the 'left' rather than the 'right', producing a Constantinian inversion without true engagement with the prior question, that of the nature of the church. The renewal of language cannot begin so long as we think that all that is to be done is to shout louder or 'apply' the language to new circumstances. It is not only that language cannot be 'applied' unless it is lived in; as the discussion of metaphor showed, language is not a tool entirely at our control, but is shaped in conversations. It is also that the 'deadness' of our language is a symptom of our historical disorientation. And so it is scarcely surprising that Christian responses to the modern world vary from puzzled perplexity, through frenetic and overpowering religiosity to an activism which tends to equate the gospel with the most worthy political causes.

One response to the situation would be that things are so bad that nothing can be done about them. In one sense, that is right: the body can be healed only by the Spirit's blowing upon dead bones and clothing them with new flesh. But to appeal to the Spirit is also an invitation to hopeful thought and activity. Theology has a part to play in such a response. It cannot itself raise the dead, but it can operate in the hope that it may have a share in the Spirit's renewing action, reviving both thought and life. The programme for this chapter, then, is to think about the church in the hope of finding a way of showing how the metaphors may return to life in a concrete community of language and life. To begin with the church is not to deny an interest in the world around. It is rather to base an enquiry in the place where the atoning grace of God is acknowledged and lived, however inadequately.

This chapter has been entitled 'The Community of Reconciliation' because it is hoped in it to show how the reconciliation between God and the world achieved on the cross may take shape in a God-given community ordered to that purpose. For the most part in the book, the word *atonement* has been preferred to reconciliation because it both calls attention to the much neglected and misunderstood substitutionary aspect of reconciliation and because *reconciliation* is a word which is overused and often trivialised. It can be saved from sentimentality if it is controlled by the metaphors and their orientation to the intractability of evil that is overcome only on the cross. We shall look at three aspects of the life of the community of reconciliation in the light of the three metaphors, but as they are interpenetrated by aspects of the other two.

II Truth

In some respects, the final completed part volume of Barth's *Church Dogmatics* is among the least satisfactory of his writings. But it was a sure instinct that led him in that book to characterise the victory of Jesus in terms of his freedom to speak the truth. We recall here some themes of Chapter 3 above: that the demonic can in part be understood in terms of slavery to the lie, involving an incapacity to distinguish truth from falsehood; that Jesus' victory took place, first of all, in a refusal to live other than by the truth (Matt.4.4: 'by every word that proceeds from the mouth of God'); that his victory took shape in his true and authoritative words, which had authority over both lies and sickness, and was completed in dying at the hands of and for the sake of those who called good evil. The lie is destroyed by the truth, which is in this case not mere words but the Word made flesh.

For the church, too, truth of life and truth of word belong together. To begin to appropriate something of the meaning of the coincidence of truth and life, we shall centre the argument on preaching or proclamation. That may appear at best rash, at worst absurd in an age when preaching is held to be in decline. Yet it continues to be testimony both to the capacity of words to be living, to make things happen, and to the mode of the divine victory which is 'not by might, nor by power, but by my Spirit' (Zech.4.6). The word is mightier than the sword, as both cross and resurrection avow. The practice of preaching is a request to the Spirit to retell the biblical narratives and promises in a new context. It takes place in the belief that the Spirit will free Jesus from past history to make his victory live in the lives and world of those who participate in the proclamation.

The fourth book of Calvin's *Institutes* is entitled, 'The external means or aims by which God invites us into the society of Christ and holds us therein'.[1] Let us pause a little to examine that word *means*. It reminds us that the Christian community lives neither in the sphere of the lie nor in the kingdom of heaven where we shall know as we are known, but 'between the times'. The victory of Jesus stands behind; its final revelation lies ahead. It is the gift of the Spirit to enable anticipations of the final victory to take place in our time. The Spirit works not by some automatic or 'magical' process, but uses *means* – earthly, this-worldly means like the humanity of Jesus – to make God's kingdom real among us.

But how can such anticipations be conceived to take place? Any community or organisation is what it is largely by virtue of the self-understanding and form of life that it embodies. In the first edition of the *Independent* newspaper, William Rees-Mogg suggested that one of the difficulties facing the B.B.C. is that it is a vast and complex institution which yet attempts to organise itself on the analogy of a cricket club. Correspondingly, the church as a community (and set of communities constituting the one catholic and apostolic church) is called to embody in that sense a particular self-understanding and form of life. One of the means of realising this call is to hold before its eyes the biblical narratives and writings which present in different ways the victory, sacrifice and justification that Jesus is. Through the Spirit the literature becomes constitutive of the life of the community, creates its self-understanding,

---

1. I owe to William Klempa the point that the reference to external means may indicate a weakness in Calvin's ecclesiology, if it suggests that the church is instrumental to the salvation of individuals within it, rather than being, as a community, part of the gospel. If so, it is a weakness which Calvin shares with much of the Western tradition (Gunton 1989), and is not intended to be repeated here.

because it is a story which sets before our eyes the action of God in the world.

It is not being suggested that preaching is the sole way of achieving that end. Baptism and the Lord's Supper are equally ways of presenting God's story before and in the community. They are, in Augustine's expression, recently taken up and expanded by R.W. Jenson (1978), visible words. Nor is it being suggested that this is all that is involved in the worship of the church. None the less, an important claim is being made, that when a community is ordered around the proclaimed victory of the Word of God, its life will, though not automatically or even always satisfactorily, take something of the shape of the victory that is celebrated: it will be *informed* by it.

III Victory

It was part of the wrong direction taken by the church in the past that crucial aspects of its narratives of institution were ignored or suppressed. We should here recall especially the words Jesus is reported to have spoken to his disciples during their dispute about greatness. 'But not so with you; rather let the greatest among you become as the youngest' (Luke 22.26). Those words, and others like them, were embodied, lived out, in Jesus' incarnation, life and death, and so become both the basis for the ordering of church and human life and a way of being in and for the world. The church's way of being is therefore necessarily a question mark to those forms of life which contradict or deny its basis and shape. Therefore John Howard Yoder is right in saying that 'Worship is the communal cultivation of an alternative construction of society and of history' (Yoder 1984 p.43). But that raises a question. How is the community that seeks to have its life formed by Jesus' way of being in the world related to those forms of life which implicitly or explicitly deny it? Here, as Yoder's analysis has shown, we require an account of the relation of church and culture which transcends the fashionable distinction between 'church' and 'sect'. That is to say, we require an ecclesiology which seeks neither to be identical with the surrounding world nor to be isolated from it: a church which is, as a distinctive community, both *in* and *for* (and therefore sometimes *against*) the world, just as Jesus was at once in, for and against the religious culture of first century Israel. In this respect, the church as a whole can profit from insights derived from the traditions of Dissent.

The reason is that, particularly in a culture which has for the most part rejected the Christian way, it is plausible to argue that only on the basis of a distinctive form of community can effective Christian life take shape in the world. Such a form need not be sectarian, for it does not follow that we should deny that the kingdom is realised in parts of 'the world' also. On the contrary, our conception of the action of God taking place by earthly means presupposes that it may happen elsewhere in the world. The point is rather that the church is called to be a parable of the kingdom of such a kind that the truth of God is visible to the world – the city set upon a hill. As Stanley Hauerwas has written, 'The social ethical task of the church... is to be the kind of community that tells and tells rightly the story of Jesus' (Hauerwas 1981 p.52). More directly to the point of this section, he says that 'the truthfulness of Jesus creates and is known by the kind of community his story should form' (p.37).

It must be remembered, however, particularly in view of the way in which the argument has taken us into the doctrine of creation, that here is more than a matter of social ethics alone. Over and above the questions of polity and society there are those perhaps prior questions which concern our living in and use of the whole order of creation. They are closely related to social ethical questions, as can be seen from one example, that of the image of God. In what sense may we understand and live the confession that the human race, male and female together, is called to embody in the world a likeness to the deity? How is it that this image is restored and perfected in Christ, the second Adam? In other words: what form of human sociality best echoes the social being of God and embodies the truth of the creation?

Similarly, many other social and ethical questions – those concerned for example with money, technology, warfare, eating and drinking, sex – are at root matters of how we inhabit and make use of the good creation of God. We may recall here Barth's use, in the posthumously published lectures which would have completed the ethical section of his fourth volume, of the concept of 'chthonic forces', lordless powers which instead of being under human control come to dominate life on earth (Barth 1976/1981 pp.227ff). 'Among these lordless powers we must certainly consider that of technology... but not that alone.' Other examples are the modern ways of fashion and of 'what is called sport': 'What is the majesty that has brought to the Olympic games the regular cultic form of worship, praise, laud, and thanksgiving?' (pp.229f). Barth has undoubtedly here put his finger on some of the slaveries of our age. They and others like them – the particular forms the demonic takes in our time – are a challenge to the Christian community's capacity to live truthfully. How far is it possible for the church to be a community that both tells the truth and enables human people to live by the truth in the world, in at least relative freedom from the idols of our time? The calling of the community of reconciliation is to be those who learn to live in the creation as creation, as gift: in the space won for the life of the world by the victory of Jesus.

Thus and only thus will it be able to open up space in which others may find freedom.

The test of the church's form of life, accordingly, is not whether it merely preaches against contemporary idolatry and lies, but whether, first, its manner of proclamation truly reveals things for what they are, idolatrous perversions of God's good creation; and, second, it develops a way of being in the world in which they are seen to be in process of defeat. The church's proclamation will be seen to be *merely* political unless its own *polity* is given shape by the victory of Christ on the cross. Here, in view of the church's vocational temptation to self-righteousness, we must remember that judgement begins with the household of God. It is, accordingly and for example, more important to shape a non-racialist form of life and a style of community in which marriages are built up and supported, than to proclaim the iniquities of others. That is not to deny the church's responsibility to the broader social order, but to urge the priority of being shaped by the victory that is God's not ours, or rather ours only because it it God's: that he, through the incarnation, cross and resurrection of Jesus creates and gives space for human life to breathe and grow.

In such a way we complete a brief survey of one way in which a metaphor of atonement may be seen to take concrete meaning, as a means of shaping the life of the church. The account requires supplementation by insights drawn from the other metaphors, and is only a beginning. The second area of belief and life will enrich the conceptual pattern which is developing.

IV   Judgement

Section II took its starting point from preaching because there is a real link between the way in which Jesus' victory is portrayed in the New Testament and his freedom to speak and be the truth. It was not intended to deny that the substance of his victory becomes real as the sacraments of baptism and the Lord's Supper speak their visible words. Like the preached word, the visible words have as their end the creation of space: or rather they are concerned with the realisation in the present of the achieved space of the atonement and the promised space of the new heaven and new earth. But the sacraments have, over and above proclamation, their own specific features. They are particular ways in which God the Spirit creates free human life. And just as victory was appropriated in terms of proclamation and truth, baptism's orientation, in continuity with Chapter 4's exploration of the justice of God, is to judgement and forgiveness. To be baptised is to undergo judgement, by accepting the work of Christ in our stead.

To say that, however, is not to deny the double focus of baptism. Baptism also symbolises cleansing: the cleansing of human life from pollution through the atoning sacrifice. It therefore sets the baptised in a community of those who, by virtue of their reconciliation to God, live their lives under the promise that they will be presented perfect before the throne of grace. But although water is a symbol of cleansing, it can be argued that of equal, and perhaps greater, weight is the fact that water is the stuff that drowns. The baptism of Jesus was his undergoing the judgement of God proclaimed by John against Israel. Therefore to undergo baptism is to accept a sentence of death, metaphorical but real. Paul makes this clear in many passages: to have been baptised is to have died with Christ. John makes a similar point in the language of rebirth (John 3). In what is perhaps his most radical assertion of the extent of Jesus' identification with the human race under judgement ('he made him to be sin who knew no sin'), Paul draws the conclusion that all have therefore died (2 Cor.5.21,15). The statement gains its force from the ontological universality of the humanity of Jesus.

Because his is the humanity of the Word through whom all things exist, his death is the death of all.

The end of baptism is, therefore, the actuality, not simply the possibility, of a new form of existence. There is 'a new act of creation' (C.K. Barrett's translation of 2 Cor.5.17, Barrett 1973 p.162). What is claimed is no more a magical transmogrification than it is literally the clinical death of the baptised. The judgement which is undergone in baptism is rather the means of entry into the living space created by the substitutionary death of Christ. Because he has undergone judgement for us and in our place, we may undergo it as a gift of life rather than as a sentence of death. But that means that it is, metaphorically but really, a sentence of death on us. Barth's claim, cited towards the end of Chapter 4, that the Son's acceptance of judgement means 'that as the people we were we have been done away with and destroyed' (Barth 1953/1956 pp.295), now comes into clearer focus. Because the Son, through whom all things come to be, is among us in the way that he is – as a man who lives a certain life and dies a certain death – certain definite implications follow for our way of being on earth.

The heart of the significance of baptism is brought out by the fact that it is baptism for the forgiveness of sins. In so speaking, we come face to face with the central problem of this section and with an opportunity to spell out what is involved in the actuality of atonement. The problem arises in the form traditionally given to baptism as the result of discussions in the Western church about sin and its relation to baptism. The doctrine of original sin developed in the West under the logic of the practice of baptising infants. Infants were baptised; baptism was for the remission of sin; therefore efforts must be made to show in what sense infants were sinful and underwent the remission of sin. As is well known, there came into prominence a doctrine that original sin was a kind of inherited stain or curse which was passed on from parent to child by means of sexual reproduction. Original sin then came to be distinguished from actual sin, so that the original was the inheritance, the actual the sinful acts performed thereafter.

While, however, the distinction between original and actual sin is an essential one, the way it was worked out was highly questionable. In the first place, sin was not treated relationally. Instead of seeing the heart of the matter in a relation between creature and creator, expressed metaphorically in terms of stain and the rest, theology tended to trace a train of historical causality back to Adam. The result was that the symptom was treated as the disease. The outcome was not only theologically problematic, but caused unnecessary difficulties for the concept of sin when historical critical scholars began to cast doubt on the existence of a historical Adam. Too much is made to hang on a chain of historical causality rather than on relations, or breach of them, with God. In the second place, the Western conception of original sin led to a tendency to operate with a dualism of inner and outer person. Original sin came to be seen as that which qualified the inner being, and was wiped away by baptism. Actual sin continued, and became the object of the disciplinary and legal structures of the church. Again, what is lost is an understanding of sin as a way of being – or of failure to be – for the whole person in relation to God and the rest of creation.

The two weaknesses correspond to a weakness in the theology of baptism and of the church. In the first place, because original sin was conceived as an invisible taint of the individual, the sacrament came to be understood as a rite, in the control of the institution, in which that stain was wiped away. It was treated individualistically, and with minimal relational content, so that the primary function of baptism, relation with God through the mediation of Christ and in the context of a living community, became secondary. The familiar definition of a sacrament as an outward and visible sign of an inward and spiritual grace betrays all the worst aspects of the syndrome. It is not much of a parody to say that the sacrament was rather like a dose of religious medicine, administered by a priest, with little sense of its being institution into a living community of worship and life. It is small wonder that the baptism of infants has come into disrepute. But the chief point here is this: that the vital link between the atonement and a living community in which it becomes concrete is lost.

We can approach the dimensions of the topic which concern us by a return to the matter of ontology. The old conception suggests, as we have seen, that there is an invisible change brought about by baptism. But because it is concerned with the removal of an *inner* stain, nothing can be seen to happen. The claim made for the sacrament naturally becomes suspect, and many have wanted to replace it with something more adequate. Sometimes an alternative has been provided by a stress on personal choice and confession. However, that, too, tends to evade the question. Does baptism do something, in the sense of bringing about some ontological change or new creation? In one sense it does not, in that its function is to signal rather than to bring about the new creation on the basis of which we are called into the church: here the change is the new birth in Christ which precedes baptism. In another sense, however, it must be possible to give some account of what it brings into being that was not there before. To develop one, we must lay on one side the distinction of inner and outer, certainly in the platonising form it has developed since Augustine, and return to a more relational conception. Baptism institutes a

187

person into a new set of personal relationships, in a community ordered around the justifying death of Christ.

In that sense, we cannot claim too much for the church, not as an institution dispensing grace, but as a community ordered to God through Christ and in the Spirit. The metaphor of the church as the body of Christ teaches that to be baptised is to be brought into relation with Christ through the community. That is something real: an ontic change, because to enter a new set of relationships – and particularly this one – is to be a new creation. Thus baptism is a way of making concrete the atonement achieved by God through Jesus. It is to enable participation in the justifying action of God. In turn, such a doctrine is definitive of the kind of community that the church is. It is the one called to live by the justice of God: accepting for itself the judgement of God on sin, borne on the cross by Jesus, so that it may in turn be the locus of transformed relationships.

V Forgiveness

The same point can be put another way by saying that to be baptised is to enter a community committed to ordering its life by the forgiveness of sins. The concept of the justice of God which has been advocated in these pages is, as we have seen, transformational rather than punitive or distributive. That is to say, it accepts human responsibility and culpability for the breach of the universal order which results from rebellion against God, but holds that justice is done not by the imposition of equivalent suffering – as we saw to be the case with 'the justice of Zeus' – but by a process of transformation in which the reconciliation of persons enables the acknowledged evil of the past to become the basis for present and future good. The notion of transformation is important because it places the essence of the matter in a renewed relation of the creation to God. It also provides the opportunity for further discussion of the form of life which is entailed by the doctrine of the atonement. We approach it with the help of classic objections which have been advanced against the doctrine by some of its pagan and Christian opponents.

In the course of its history, the Christian understanding of the atonement has come under the accusation of injustice – of flying in the face of moral reality. One form of the objection was made against Origen by Celsus, that by teaching forgiveness the church undermines morality. 'Every other religion, he complains, invites only the blameless, the educated, the respectable; Christianity actually seems to put a premium on wrong-doing, so cordially does it welcome the evil and debased' (Mackintosh 1934 p.19, compare the similar charge made by the Socinians, Harnack 1885/1899 p.158). Whatever the historical truth of such a claim, it does point to a fundamental difficulty. If God forgives sins, does it follow that behaviour does not matter? Paul had already faced the question in his discussion of justification. 'Are we to continue in sin that grace may abound?' (Rom. 6.1). His reply to his own question is not couched, it must be noted, in abstract discussions of legality, but consists of an appeal to the way things are in the church. The preaching that Christ is our substitute under the justice of God does not undermine morality, but establishes it. Paul has been quite explicit at an earlier stage of his argument. 'Do we then overthrow the law by this faith? By no means! On the contrary, we uphold the law' (3.31). The concrete basis for his defence of the gospel is, however, to be found in his discussion of baptism. In baptism, new realities have been established. 'We were buried with (Christ) by baptism unto death' (6.4); 'let not sin therefore reign in your mortal bodies' (6.12). Baptism has set the baptised in a new relation with God in which is instituted a process of living out of the destructive past into the inaugurated and promised redemption (6.5).

The form of life which follows is that which takes shape from its movement between past atonement and promised redemption. Theology sometimes speaks too easily of the wiping out of the past, as if the whole of salvation has already happened. In one sense, it has: the death of Christ for the forgiveness of sins is once-for-all and complete. One has died for all, and therefore all have died. But, as we have already seen, the past event has to be realised and lived. Forgiveness is therefore about being placed in a position – in the life of a community – where the evil past can be acknowledged while at the same time being used as basis for a new form of life; where it can be atoned because it has been atoned. The metaphor of space has been used in this book as a way of characterising what God gives in the atonement. But we could also speak in terms of time. God gives time to those who are incorporate in Christ. Forgiveness, on such an account, is about the free acknowledgement of offences alongside a refusal to allow them to define the future of relationships. On such an understanding, those who share baptism will form a community that lives on such a basis. The form of life shaped by the gospel will then involve the acknowledgement of faults before God and each other alongside confession that the basis for human living is to be found in a common incorporation into the body of Christ. To enter the church is therefore to enter a form of community in which the vicarious suffering of Jesus becomes the basis for a corresponding form of life, one in which the offence of others is borne rather than avenged.

Such a theology of the church is not, however, to be treated as a self-contained truth, unrelated to life in 'the world', because it contains elements of universal moral truth. The truth about Christian claims for forgiveness is revealed in the fact that forgiveness is creative of human moral possibilities in the way that the alternative, a doctrine of the absolute requirement of punishment and vengeance, is not. There is, indeed, a kind of 'natural justice' in vengeance, even in the vendetta. But the gospel is that the cycle of offence and retribution is broken only by something different: by the creative re-establishment of human relations on a new basis. True reconciliation in that sense cannot ignore the past, which otherwise continues to spread its poison. (That is why it is often asserted that there can be no true reconciliation in Ireland until the English confess their share of culpability for the way things are.) The ethical task of the community of the forgiven follows directly from this. It is to live the justice of God made real by Jesus' bearing of the consequences of human injustice. It is therefore to live the life of the age to come in the present.

But if the first task is to embody a certain form of life, is there a second? What is the bearing of this form of life on that which the world calls justice? Again, we must discuss the question as it reaches us through the tradition. One chief answer has tended to be given, in two different forms. It is that the task of the church is to impose, so far as it can, the justice of God upon the structures of the kingdoms of this world. The two forms the answer takes depend upon distinct construals of the word *justice*. The approach which has ruled for much of Christendom, East as well as West, holds that the justice of God is to be realised in the upholding of the order of creation. Especially when that order is taken to be something laid down in the past, the church will see its task as the support of the established social order. (That is not necessarily a 'reactionary' task: the order laid down can equally well be conceived to be a 'revolutionary' one.)

The second construal of justice is oriented more to a theology of redemption than creation, and stresses the need for a new social order involving juster economic and social arrangements. It is, as is well known, the approach increasingly favoured by the mainstream churches, despite widespread undercurrents of dissatisfaction, and can certainly claim a large measure of biblical support. Its chief danger, however, is similar to the danger of the once preferred conception and that is of what can be called a 'Constantinian inversion'. On the rebound from a history of reactionary involvement, the Christian community may commit itself to particular political programmes whose methods and therefore outcome are not very different from those of the past. One secularisation of the gospel will therefore be replaced by another (see Neuhaus 1984).

How should we respond, within the terms of this book, to such alternative conceptions of justice? On the one hand, it may not be denied that there is an analogy between divine and human political justice in which the poor are lifted up and the prisoner released. Indeed, there is more than an analogy, for the justice of God achieves such transformations wherever they take place, by whomsoever they are brought about. The justice of God realised in Christ is universal justice. On the other hand, however, there are necessary differences between the way in which the justice of God is achieved in Christ – by the refusal to exercise coercion – and by the way in which fallen human societies, both those claiming a 'Christian' basis and others, tend to realise it. The justice of God is transforming action achieved through the crucifixion of Jesus. God's power is exercised in weakness.

To say that, however, is not to deny that the crucifixion was a political act, in the sense of an act whose context was a struggle about and for true human polity. As Alasdair

Heron has remarked, we must remember that Jesus 'was not crucified on an altar between two candles, but on Golgotha between two thieves' (Heron 1980 p.168). The question is not whether the Christian community has any responsibility for the society within which its life takes shape, but what that responsibility is and how it is expressed. An essential beginning should be made in the claim that, if it is the eternal Word, through whom all things have their being, who conquers on the cross, then there can be no other basis for society than that given it in Christ. 'If such an one died for all, in that act all died. It therefore commits Society to a development to that holy end' (Forsyth 1962 p.20). All human social life has its basis in redemption, whether it is prepared to acknowledge it or not. The church's being, acts and words therefore fulfil its responsibility to society when they are directed to that end alone. The primary task is not to organise the world, but to be within it as a particular way of being human, a living reminder of the true basis and end of human life.

There is, at present, some doubt whether that end is being sought in the right way. The tendency of the church in recent times has been to lecture the state on social justice. Lecturing may be necessary, but it is empty if nothing else underlies and confirms it. To quote Forsyth again: 'Christ's action on the world is not preceptual... Precepts may be but local, temporary, individual. And they always tend to become either casuistic or out of date... Christ's supreme eternal work is in His cross' (p.17). The Christian community is there to remind the state that political and moral programmes are secondary to and dependent upon redemption. There is reconciliation and justice only through the judgement of God and the cross of Christ that lead to repentance and forgiveness: only through the creative transformation of relationships.

To return to the main theme of this chapter, we must recall that it concerns the way in which the dry bones of the traditional metaphors of atonement may take on living flesh. It will happen only when they are endowed with new life by the Spirit. The new life may, however, be requested and sought actively, by a return to the source of the language in the story of Jesus who is the justice of God in the world. There is no technique for achieving such an end, but if the judgement and reconciliation of God do take shape in Jesus, are we not bound to trust that, even and especially in times where the language has lost its force, it will be renewed for those who are faithful? The chief mark which distinguishes the church from other institutions and societies is that it lives from the atonement, that 'happy exchange' which frees it from pleading its own moral success. Such life as it has is the gift of God the Spirit, bringing the baptised ever and again in Christ to the Father.

Two things remain to be said to take us into the next section. They concern topics which the present section leaves unsaid. The first is that it will be recalled (above, Chapter 4, Section V) that the justice of God is not to be construed in merely personalistic terms, but in terms of God's active loyalty to the created order as a whole. We have seen that God's active loyalty to the social order is expressed through the universal basis of social life in Christ and the church as it is called to concrete realisation of its form of life under judgement. Thus far, an attempt has been made to undermine the individualism of the concept and practice of baptism. Nothing has been said directly, however, of the wider, cosmic, dimensions of the justifying work of God. There is no doubt that proper respect for the created order as a whole is one of the responsibilities laid upon the church both by the victory of Jesus over the demonic and by his submission to judgement. But the theme will be more appropriately dealt with in the section to come.

The second concluding remark is that, while baptism is the means by which the Christian is *instituted* into a new set of relationships, the atonement takes concrete form in other ways than that once-for-all orientation to the cross and resurrection of Jesus. A further dimension of the church's life is its continued constitution as a community of the faithful. Such a theme takes us directly into a treatment of our third major theme, in which an attempt is made to appropriate some of the riches of the metaphor of sacrifice.

VI Community

The doctrine of the Lord's Supper has, even more than that of baptism, been turned into a clerically controlled rite in which a sacrament is administered to individuals, as medicine by a physician. Indicative of the conceptual chaos which reigns is the development of expressions which fit the medical analogy, like 'receiving' communion. Can this really be what is meant by 'the medicine of immortality' or should we seek a more adequate construction of the metaphor? Such would stress the fact that communion is koinonia, community; and with that there comes a change of emphasis, from the individual's communion with God, which does not have to be denied in its proper place, to the community's participating in the wedding feast of the lamb.

The structure of much modern worship serves only to reinforce the individualistic interpretation. Despite the development of liturgies more expressive of communal celebration, many modern rites are in other ways inimical to communion. The trail to the altar rail accentuates both individual reception and the class division between active clergy and receptive laity; while in free church liturgy, despite many salutary developments, the manner of distribution maintains the tradition of nineteenth century individualism. What is lacking is a crucial link joining the atonement and the life of the community as a whole in the context of which the celebration takes place. The deficiency is ecclesiological: we lack a conception of the church as the space in which God gives community with himself and so between human people.

When we survey the depressing history of ecclesiological thought, the dimensions of the problem become plainer. The background is to be found in the tendency to conceive salvation as something handed to the apostles – unhistorically seen as the first 'clergy' – which is then mediated to the people through an institutional élite. In place of a community, there developed a hierarchy. A similar point emerges in terms of the doctrine of the Holy Spirit. Rather than being conceived as God in his eschatological action of constituting the community of the age to come, the Spirit came to be depersonalised and treated as a force (causally) empowering an already given community: moving the institution into action. In place of this we need, as John Zizioulas has argued, a conception of the church as indeed *instituted* by Christ, but requiring *constitution* in every new present by the Spirit (Zizioulas 1985 p.132). The time-honoured and sometimes time-worn emphasis on the church's relation to God in its past, mediated through the institutional structure, needs to be relativised by an emphasis on the present action of God the Spirit mediated through the life of the community as a whole.

We shall begin a reshaping of the conceptuality of communion by a return to the metaphor of sacrifice. It is, in the first place, clear that there is in the various New Testament accounts of the institution of the Lord's Supper a strong emphasis on sacrifice. Paul, Mark and Matthew alike link the cup with the covenant and with death, deliberately relating Jesus' death with an earlier covenantal sacrifice (1 Cor.11.25ff, Mark 14.24, Matt.26.28, cf Exod.24.8); while Luke and almost certainly John make a direct link with the passover (Luke 22.15, John 19.14). Such differences as there are between the accounts are important in revealing the metaphorical character of the usages. They are not used in slavish dependence upon Old Testament meanings, but freely take up such aspects as enable the authors to draw out in different ways the redemptive significance of the event. It is one of the tragedies of church history that slavish use of categories, in the service of institutional ideology, insisted that the church's celebration of the event was literally a sacrifice. The point for us, however, is that the accounts of the institution of the sacrament do use sacrificial language but do so in the context of the other metaphors of atonement. Thus Paul links sacrifice with judgement and so, we might say, the eucharist with a renewal of baptism. In his somewhat obscure pastoral application of the words of institution he clearly implies a relation between celebration and judgement and, when it is duly celebrated, with salutary (transformative) judgement: 'when we are judged by the Lord we are chastened' (1 Cor.11.32). Similarly, Luke's use of passover rather than covenantal language links the supper with liberation, thus forming the obverse of his concern to show that the encounter with the demonic comes to a head in the passion of Jesus (see 22.40, 23.35-7).

In following up the implications of the narratives of institution, we must remember that the metaphor of sacrifice is at once the richest and the most difficult to handle conceptually – as the vagaries of church history again indicate – because, of all the language, it brings us closest not only to the historic action of God in Christ, but to the heart of his very being. Such a claim indeed justifies the concern that the church has always had for the integrity and centrality of the Lord's Supper (even though it has not always maintained them in the right way). It is not only, as is often pointed out – though the irony should be noted – the sacrament of unity; it is also the place where its community, in the image of the community that God is, is constituted by the Spirit who realises the presence of Christ anew in his world. When all this is said, however, the caveat already made in this section should be repeated. The actual shape the church's life and worship have taken is often a practical denial of such claims, making them appear the product of false consciousness. The challenge therefore recurs. Can the central conceptuality be reshaped under the impact of the historic sacrifice in such a way that the claims appear less hollow?

The sacrifice of Jesus, as we saw, must be understood on two levels. It is, on the one hand, the concentrated self-giving of God through the birth, life, death and resurrection of his incarnate Son. The Son, by a complete identification of himself with the world, even to death, does the work of the Father, and so mediates his eternal love for the world in the face of, and in order to heal, the world's evil. It is in that sense that it is necessary to speak of the lamb slain from the foundation of the world. However, in so speaking we do not peddle some mythology of a suffering God, but a theology of the (concentrated) taking place in time of the eternal and loving world-directness of God the Son, taking form as the expression of the freedom of God to be both himself and incarnate for us. In that sense, all that Jesus does is the concentrated action of God: the taking place of the life of God, as love and judgement, in, with and for the world. On the other hand, at another level Jesus' sacrifice is, through the action of the Spirit, the concentrated offering of human life to the Father. To say that it is the Son's life is to say that it is representative of all life. The incarnate Son pours out his life so that the Spirit may lift unredeemed life into communion with God. Jesus is thus at once the realisation of the communion of creator with creature and of creature with creator.

The ecclesiological outcome, so to speak, is that the work of Christ and the Spirit is to create, in time and space, a living echo of the communion that God is in eternity. There emerges a notion of the church as the community that is created and called to be the finite embodiment of the eternal communion of Father, Son and Spirit. The conception is one that has been more influential in the thought of Eastern Orthodoxy than in the various strains of Western Christianity, for a number of reasons, among them the greater stress laid by the East on the doctrine of the Trinity and that by the West on the legal-institutional aspects of ecclesiology. The latter in its turn has helped to shape the dominance in Western liturgies of notions of sin and forgiveness, at the expense of a stress on both community and the wider dimensions of life in the world. Here we take up the theme promised at the end of the previous section, where it was recalled that the justifying work of God is directed not to human life alone, but to that in the context of God's loyalty to the whole creation. That dimension is taken up in a notion of communion which bursts the limits of human community, and spills over into the rest of the world. 'The eucharist is the great sacrifice of praise by which the Church speaks on behalf of the whole creation... (it) opens up the vision of the divine rule which has been promised as the final renewal of creation' (World Council of Churches 1982 4.22).

Again, we can only adumbrate the implications for the life of a community gathered around the Lord's Table. It has already been argued that the first calling of the church is the creation of reconciled forms of community, both for their own sake and for the sake of human community in general, as reflections of God's movement into the world in the incarnation. Human community is the gift of the God who is himself communion. The church is called to be the echo of the very being of God, and is enabled to be so as it is taken up in worship into the life of the Trinity. But there is now something to be added to the themes of previous sections, and that is a responsibility for the life of creation as a whole, so that it too at its own level and in its own way may share in the reconciliation of all things in Christ.

We are often reminded of the ecological crisis that is the product of human misuse of the creation. There is no need to repeat here an obvious lesson for those who proclaim the renewal of all things. But what, apart from pious moralising and an increased awareness of responsibility for the creation, has the theology of the atonement to contribute? How do we share in the task of realising the achieved cleansing of the created order from the pollution visited upon it by our misuse?

VII Praise

To seek an answer to that question, we move to another word that is used to describe the Lord's Supper, the eucharist or thanksgiving. As we have seen, the Lima document describes the eucharist as 'a great sacrifice of praise', praise on behalf of the whole creation. May it not be suggested, accordingly, that the church's primary way of embodying the sacrifice of Jesus is – consistently with the early metaphorical use of the word *sacrifice* in the Psalms (noted in Chapter 5, Section II) – as a community of praise? In one sense, the church has nothing else to do but praise, when that word is used to characterise not just the particular acts we call worship, but a whole way of being in the world.

The centrality of praise both for theology and for the life of the church has been spelled out recently in Daniel Hardy and David Ford's *Jubilate. Theology in Praise* (1984). Some of their opening remarks indicate that praise is the very word for the human response to the atonement. 'Praise is... an attempt to cope with the abundance of God's love' (p.1). 'Praise perfects perfection' (p.6). It has already been remarked that when we explore the death of Jesus with the assistance of the language of sacrifice we come to the heart of the being of God, to his perfection (Chapter 5, Section IV). From one point of view – christologically – the sacrifice is perfect, complete, once for all. All that is needed for salvation has been done. But from another – pneumatologically – in the praise of word and life that perfection awaits perfection. Therefore, to return to *Jubilate*, we must understand basic Christian existence as praise (pp.71ff). 'If life is the process of self-refinement which occurs in praise, and if the condition for this occurs when the excellent-in-itself is present, it can be said that the praise of God actually constitutes the life which we live' (p.157).

Those who are sceptical about the value of the worship of God sometimes make remarks about the inappropriateness of supposing that the deity has the infinite appetite for congratulation that the activity sometimes seems to require. But that is to miss the point entirely. Praise perfects perfection: it is the movement out of self into free and glad relationship with the other. To be truly human is, it must be realised, not to be curved in upon ourselves (one of Luther's definitions of sin) but to be liberated from self-preoccupation by and to the praise of God and each other. That is not to deny or evade the existence of sin and death. The theology of the atonement is, as we have seen, the theology of God's redeeming involvement in the worst of our evil. 'Praise of God celebrates his identification of himself through the crucifixion and resurrection of Jesus' (Hardy and Ford p.106). The praise of God is the style of the life which moves from perfected reconciliation to promised victory.

The scriptures, and particularly the Psalms, are witness to the way in which the whole of creation shares in the human praise of God. It would be a grave mistake, a sign of a captivity to outmoded mechanistic views of the universe, to dismiss such expressions as fanciful and primitive. Our ecological crisis has come about in large part because we have treated the world not as creation but as inert mechanism. It is the church's calling, as the community of praise, to share in the creation's liberation from the bondage to decay so that it may obtain the glorious liberty of the children of God. Our worship is incomplete unless it offers to the creator, from the midst of our demonised world, the firstfruits of the creation liberated to praise its Lord. The eschatological visions of deserts blooming and lions lying down with lambs are not nostalgia for lost paradise, but concrete depictions of what in the Spirit may come to pass. The use of bread, wine and water in worship represent such transformations. Discussions of the real presence of Christ in the bread and wine become arid and scholastic in the worst sense unless they are controlled by a conception of the Spirit's redemption of all things in Christ.

In his celebration of the music of Mozart, Peter Shaffer puts the following words into the mouth of his composer:

> I tell you I want to write a finale lasting half an hour! A quartet becoming a quintet becoming a sextet. On and on, wider and wider – all sounds multiplying and rising together – and the together making a sound entirely new!... I bet you that's how God hears the world. Millions of sounds ascending at once and mixing in His ear to become an unending music, unimaginable to us! (Shaffer 1981 p. 70)

If such a statement is not to appear to evade the reality of evil, it must be construed christologically. God hears the world as praise in Christ, by virtue of his sacrifice. The church's praise is true worship when the Spirit empowers it to offer the first fruits of the redeemed creation to the Father, in water, bread and wine, and, more generally, in word and music. The Eastern tradition of Christian theology can express this in ways which have much to teach us:

> What the hymnographers heard, their pens brought down to earth, enabling the Church to sing in harmony with the angelic choirs. This was the leitourgia (lit. function) of the hymnographer, i.e. to unite earth to heaven in one melodious cosmic hymn of praise to the Creator. No troparion contains a single static line. Everywhere there is light, movement and music. Heaven and earth sing together, past and present merge. Eden and Bethlehem become one. The universe is one. All the hymns reveal the eternal and dynamic encounter between God and humanity. We are shown the wholly human response to that mystery which has come upon us, which is beyond ourselves, and yet towards which we strain. (Timiadis 1985 pp. 40f)

Isaac Watts, too, knew something of the eschatological unity of nature and grace, realised in the atoning sacrifice and celebrated in the church's worship. Let him have the last word:

> The whole creation join in one
>> To bless the sacred name
> Of him who sits upon the throne
>> And to adore the lamb.

REFERENCES AND BIBLIOGRAPHY

Anselm of Canterbury *Why God became Man*, E.T. of *Cur Deus Homo* by E.R. Fairweather, in *A Scholastic Miscellany: Anselm to Ockham. Library of Christian Classics* X, London: SCM Press, 1956

Aulén, Gustav (1931/1970) *Christus Victor. An Historical Study of the Three Main Types of the Idea of the Atonement.* E.T. by A.G. Hebert, London: SPCK

Baillie, D.M. (1956) *God Was in Christ. An Essay in Incarnation and Atonement.* London: Faber

Balthasar, H.U. von (1967/1982) *The Glory of the Lord. A Theological Aesthetics. I. Seeing the Form.* E.T. by E. Leiva–Merikakis, Edinburgh: T.&T. Clark

Balthasar, H.U. von (1969/1984) *The Glory of the Lord. A Theological Aesthetics. II. Studies in Theological Style: Clerical Styles.* E.T. by Andrew Louth and others, Edinburgh: T. & T. Clark

Barnett, C.K. (1962) *A Commentary on the Epistle to the Romans.* London: A. & C. Black

Barrett, C.K. (1973) *A Commentary on the Second Epistle to the Corinthians.* London: A.& C. Black

Barth, J.R. (1969) *Coleridge and Christian Doctrine.* Cambridge, Mass: Harvard University Press

Barth, Karl (1945/1958) *Church Dogmatics III/1.* E.T. edited by G.W. Bromiley and T.F. Torrance, Edinburgh: T.& T. Clark

Barth, Karl (1952/1972) *Protestant Theology in the Nineteenth Century. Its Background and History.* E.T. by Brian Cozens and John Bowden, London: SCM

Barth, Karl (1953/1956) *Church Dogmatics IV/1*

Barth, Karl (1959/1961) *Church Dogmatics IV/3*

Barth, Karl (1976/1981) *The Christian Life. Church Dogmatics IV/4, Lecture Fragments*. E.T. by Geoffrey Bromiley, Grand Rapids: Eerdmans

Barth, Markus (1961) *Was Christ's Death a Sacrifice?* Edinburgh: Oliver and Boyd

Berggren, Douglas (1962-3) 'The Use and Abuse of Metaphor', *Review of Metaphysics* 16.2, pp.237-58; 16.3, pp.450-72

Bernstein, Richard (1985) *Beyond Objectivism and Relativism. Science, Hermeneutics and Praxis*. Philadelphia: University of Pennsylvania Press

Black, Max (1962) *Models and Metaphors*. New York: Cornell University Press

Boothe, Wayne C. (1974) *Modern Dogma and the Rhetoric of Assent*. Chicago and London: University of Chicago Press

Boyd, Richard (1979) 'Metaphor and Theory Change: What is "Metaphor" a Metaphor for?', *Metaphor and Thought*, ed. A. Ortony, Cambridge University Press, pp.356-408

Brauch, M.T. (1977) 'Perspectives on "God's Righteousness" in Recent German Discussion', in E.P. Sanders (1977), pp. 523-42

Brown, Colin (1978) 'Sacrifice', in *New Internatinal Dictionary of New Testament Theology*. Exeter: Paternoster Press, 1978

Brunner, Emil (1947) *The Mediator. A Study of the Central Doctrine of the Christian Faith*. E.T. by Olive Wyon, Philadelphia: Westminster Press

Buren, Paul van (1957) *Christ in our Place. The Substitutionary Character of Calvin's Doctrine of Reconciliation*. Edinburgh: Oliver and Boyd

Caird, G.B. (1956) *Principalities and Powers*. Oxford: Clarendon Press

Caird, G.B. (1966) *A Commentary on the Revelaton of St John the Divine*. London: A. & C. Black

Caird. G.B. (1980) *The Language and Imagery of the Bible*. London: Duckworth

Calvin, John (1549/1853) *Commentaries on the Epistle of Paul the Apostle to the Hebrews*. E.T. by J. Owen, Edinburgh: Calvin Translation Society

REFERENCES AND BIBLIOGRAPHY

Camfield, F.W. (1948) 'The Idea of Substitution in the Doctrine of the Atonement.' *Scottish Journal of Theology* 1, pp. 282-293

Campbell, J. Mcleod (1856) *The Nature of the Atonement and its Relation to Remission of Sins and Eternal Life.* 5th edition, London: Macmillan, 1878

Carr, Wesley (1981) *Angels and Principalities. The Background, Meaning and Development of the Pauline phrase, 'hai archai kai hai exousiai'.* Cambridge University Press

Dalferth, I.U. (1981) *Religiöse Rede von Gott.* Munich: Christian Kaiser

Davies, Douglas (1982) Article Review: 'Sacrifice in Theology and Anthropology.' *Scottish Journal of Theology* 35 (1982), pp.351-358

Davison, Donald (1978) 'What Metaphors Mean.' *Critical Enquiry* 5, pp.31-47

de Man, Paul (1978) 'The Epistemology of Metaphor.' *Critical Enquiry* 5, pp.13-30

Denney, James (1902/1950) *The Death of Christ.* London: Tyndale Press

Dillistone, F.W. (1968/1984) *The Christian Understanding of Atonement.* London: SCM Press

Dobbie, Robert (1958) 'Sacrifice and Morality in the Old Testament.' *Expository Times* 70, pp.297-300

Dodds, E.R. (1951) *The Greeks and the Irrational.* London: University of California Press

Douglas, Mary (1984) *Purity and Danger. An Analysis of the Concepts of Pollution and Taboo.* London: Ark Books (1ᵉ1966)

Dunlop, A.I. (1960) 'Christ's Sacrifice for Sin.' *Scottish Journal of Theology* 13, pp. 383-393

Dunn, J.D.G. (1974) 'Paul's Understanding of the Death of Jesus.' *Reconciliation and Hope. New Testament Essays on Atonement and Eschatology*, edited by R.J. Banks, Exeter: Paternoster Press, pp.125-141

Emmet, Dorothy (1979) *The Moral Prism.* London: Macmillan

Fackenheim, Emil (1967) *The Religious Dimension in Hegel's Thought.* Bloomington and London: Indiana U.P.

Fairweather, ER. (1961) 'Incarnation and Atonement. An Anselmian Response to Aulén's *Christus Victor.' Canadian Journal of Theology* 7, pp.167-175

Field, Hartry (1973) 'Theory Change and the Indeterminacy of Reference.' *Journal of Philosophy* 70, pp.462-481

Fitzmyer, J.A. (1975) 'Reconciliation in Pauline Theology.' *No Famine in the Land. Studies in Honour of John L. MacKenzie*, edited by J.W. Flanagan and A.W. Robinson, Missoula: Scholars Press, pp. 155-77

Forsyth, P.T. (1909/1948) *The Cruciality of the Cross.* London: Independent Press

Forsyth, P.T. (1916) *The Justification of God.* London: Duckworth

Forsyth, P.T. (1962) *The Church, the Gospel and Society.* London: Independent Press

Frei, Hans (1974) *The Eclipse of Biblical Narrative. A Study in Eighteenth and Nineteenth Century Hermeneutics.* Yale U.P.

Frei, Hans (1975) *The Identity of Jesus Christ.* Philadelphia: Fortress Press

Geach, P.T. (1987) 'Reference and Buridan's Law', *Philosophy* 62, pp. 7-15

Goodman, Nelson (1969) *Languages of Art. An Approach to a Theory of Symbols.* Oxford University Press

Grant, Colin (1986) 'The Abandonment of Atonement.' *King's Theological Review* 9, pp. 1-8

Gunton, Colin E. (1977) 'The Biblical Understanding of Reconciliation: Paul and Jacob before God.' *Free Church Chronicle* 32, pp.17-22

Gunton, Colin E. (1985a) 'Christus Victor Revisited. A Study in Metaphor and the Transformation of Meaning.' *Journal of Theological Studies* 36, pp.129-145

Gunton, Colin E. (1985b) 'The Justice of God.' *Free Church Chronicle* 40, pp. 13-19

Gunton, Colin E. (1987) 'Christ the Sacrifice. Aspects of the Language and Imagery of the Bible.' *The Glory of Christ in the New Testament,* edited by L.D. Hurst and N.T. Wright, Oxford University Press, pp. 229-238

REFERENCES AND BIBLIOGRAPHY

Gunton, Colin E. (1989) 'The Church on Earth. The Roots of Community.' *On Being the Church. Essays on the Christian Community*, edited by C.E. Gunton and D.W. Hardy, Edinburgh: T. & T. Clark

Hardy, D.W. and Ford, D.F. (1984) *Jubilate. Theology in Praise*. London: Darton, Longman and Todd

Harnack, Adolf (1885/1896) *History of Dogma. Vol. II*. E.T. of 3ᶜ by Neil Buchanan, London: Williams and Norgate

Harnack, Adolf (1885/1897) *History of Dogma. Vol. III*. E.T. by J. Millar

Harnack, Adolf (1885/1899) *History of Dogma. Vol. VII*. E.T. by W. M'Gilchrist

Hauerwas, Stanley (1981) *A Community of Character. Towards a Constructive Christian Social Ethic*. University of Notre Dame Press

Hegel, G.W.F. (1895) *Lectures on the Philosophy of Religion*. E.T. by E.B. Speirs and J.B. Sanderson, London: Kegan Paul, Trench Trubner

Hengel, Martin (1981) *The Atonement. A Study of the Origins of the Doctrine in the New Testament*. London: SCM Press

Heron, Alasdair (1980) *A Century of Protestant Theology*. London: Lutterworth

Hesse, Mary (1966) 'The Explanatory Function of Metaphor.' *Models and Analogies in Science*, University of Notre Dame Press, pp.157-177

Hobbes, Thomas (1651/1962) *Leviathan: or the Matter, Forme and Power of a Commonwealth, Ecclesiasticall and Civil*, ed. Michael Oakeshott, London: Collier Macmillan

Irving, Edward (1828/1865) *The Collected Writings of Edward Irving in Five Volumes, Vol. V*. Edited by G. Carlyle, London: Alexander Strahan

Irving, Edward (1828) *The Last Days. A Discourse on the Evil Character of these our times: Proving them to be the 'Perilous Times' of the 'Last Days'*. London: Seeley and Burnside

Jenson, R.W. (1978) *Visible Words. The Interpretation and Practice of Christian Sacraments*. Philadelphia: Fortress Press

Jüngel, Eberhard (1974) 'Metaphorisches Wahrheit. Erwägungen zur theologischen Relevanz der Metapher als Beitrag zur Hermeneutik einer narrativen Theologie', in P. Ricoeur and E. Jüngel, *Metapher, Zur Hermeneutik religiser Sprache,* Munich: Christian Kaiser, pp.71-122

Kant, Immanuel (1793/1951) *Critique of Judgement.* E.T. by J.H. Bernard, London: Collier Macmillan

Kant, Immanuel (1794/1960) *Religion Within the Limits of Reason Alone.* E.T. by T.M. Greene and H.H. Hudson, New York: Harper and Row

Kasper, Walter (1974/1976) *Jesus the Christ.* E.T. by V. Green, London: Burns and Oates

Kierkegaard, Søren (1843/1959) *Either/Or.* E.T. by D.F. Swenson and L.M. Swenson, New York: Anchor Books

Kripke, Saul (1980) *Naming and Necessity*, 2nd edition, Oxford: Blackwell

Lakoff, G. and Johnson, Mark (1980) *Metaphors We Live By.* London: University of Chicago Press

Lloyd Jones, Hugh (1971) *The Justice of Zeus.* London: University of California Press

Locke, John (1690/1959) *An Essay Concerning Human Understanding. Book III: Of Words.* New York: Dover

Luther, Martin (1545/1960) *Preface to the Complete Edition of Luther's Latin Writings, Wittenberg 1545.* In *Works, vol 34.* Edited by Lewis H. Spitz, Philadelphia: Muhlenberg Press

McCloskey, Mary A. (1964) 'Metaphors.' *Mind* 73, pp.215-233

McFague, Sallie (1983) *Metaphorical Theology. Models of God in Religious Language.* London: SCM Press

McGrath, Alister (1986) *Justitia Dei. A History of the Christian Doctrine of Justification.* Two vols., Cambridge University Press

MacKinnon, D.M. (1966) 'Subjective and Objective Conceptions of Atonement.' *Prospect for Theology. Essays in Honour of H.H. Farmer*, edited by F.G. Healey, Welwyn: Nisbet

Mackintosh, H.R. (1934) *The Christian Experience of Forgiveness.* London: Nisbet

REFERENCES AND BIBLIOGRAPHY

McIntyre, John (1954) *St Anselm and his Critics. A Re-interpretation of the Cur Deus Homo.* Edinburgh and London: Oliver and Boyd

Mallow, V.R. (1983) *The Demonic. A Selected Theological Study. An Examination into the Theology of Edwin Lewis, Karl Barth and Paul Tillich.* London: University Press of America

Manson, T.W. (1945) 'Hilasterion.' *Journal of Theological Studies* 46, pp. 1-4

Martin, Ralph P. (1981) *Reconciliation. A Study of Paul's Theology.* London: Marshall, Morgan and Scott

May, Rollo (1970) *Love and Will.* London: Collins

Moberly, R.C. (1901) *Atonement and Personality.* London: John Murray

Neuhaus, R.J. (1984) *The Naked Public Square. Religion and Democracy in America.* Grand Rapids: Eerdmans

Olsen, Glenn W. (1981) 'Hans Urs von Balthasar and the Rehabilitation of St. Anselm's Doctrine of the Atonement.' *Scottish Journal of Theology* 34 pp.49-61

Parker, Robert (1984) *Miasma. Pollution and Purification in Early Greek Religion.* Oxford University Press

Paul, Robert S. (1961) *The Atonement and the Sacraments. The Relation of the Atonement to the Sacraments of Baptism and the Lord's Supper.* London: Hodder and Stoughton

Ricoeur, Paul (1977) *The Rule of Metaphor. Multidisciplinary Studies of the Creation of Meaning in Language.* E.T. by R. Czerny and others, Toronto and Buffalo: University of Toronto Press

Rogerson, J.W. (1980) 'Sacrifice in the Old Testament: Problems of Method and Approach' in *Sacrifice,* edited by M.F.C. Bourdillon and M. Fortes, London: Academic Press, pp.45-59

Rowley, H.H. (1959) 'Sacrifice and Morality: A Rejoinder.' *Expository Times* 70 pp.341-342

Sanders, E.P. (1977) *Paul and Palestinian Judaism.* London: SCM Press

Schleiermacher, F.D.E. (1830/1928) *The Christian Faith.* E.T. by H.R. Mackintosh and J.S. Stewart, Edinburgh: T. & T. Clark

Shaffer, Peter (1981) *Amadeus.* London: Penguin Books

Sölle, Dorothee (1965/1967) *Christ the Representative. An Essay in Theology after the 'Death of God'*. E.T. by D. Lewis, London: SCM Press

Soskice, Janet Martin (1985) *Metaphor and Religious Language*. Oxford University Press

Stanford, W. Bedell (1936) *Greek Metaphor*. Oxford: Blackwell

Steiner, George (1975) *After Babel. Aspects of Language and Translation*. Oxford University Press

Surin, Kenneth (1982) 'Atonement and Christology.' *Neue Zeitschrift für Systematische Theologie und Religionsphilosophie* 24 pp.131-149

Surin, Kenneth (1986) *Theology and the Problem of Evil*. Oxford: Blackwell

Sutherland, Stewart R. (1978) 'Language and Interpretation in Crime and Punishment.' *Philosophy and Literature*, pp.223-236

Swain, C.W. (1963) '"For our Sins". The Image of Sacrifice in the Thought of the Apostle Paul.' *Interpretation* 7, pp.131-139

Sykes, S.W. (1980) 'Sacrifice in the New Testament and Christian Theology.' In *Sacrifice*, details under Rogerson (1980), pp.61-83

Taylor, Vincent (1941) *Forgiveness and Reconciliation. A Study in New Testament Theology*. London: Macmillan

Thiemann, Ronald F. (1985) *Revelation and Theology. The Gospel as Narrated Promise*. Notre Dame: University of Notre Dame Press

Tillich, Paul (1968) *Systematic Theology. Combined Volume.* London: Nisbet

Timiadis, Emilianos (1985) 'God's Immutability and Communicability'. *Theological Dialogue between Orthodox and Reformed Churches*, ed. by T.F. Torrance, Edinburgh and London: Scottish Academic Press, pp. 23-49

Tracy, David (1978) 'Metaphor and Religion: the Test Case of Christian Texts.' *Critical Enquiry* 5, pp.91-106

Turbayne, C.M. (1970) *The Myth of Metaphor*. Columbia: University of South Carolina Press, 2nd edition

Wallace, R.S. (1981) *The Atoning Death of Christ*. London: Marshall, Morgan and Scott

REFERENCES AND BIBLIOGRAPHY

Weingart, R.E. (1970) *The Logic of Divine Love. A Critical Analysis of the Soteriology of Peter Abailard*. Oxford: Clarendon Press

Wells, David F. (1978) *The Search for Salvation*. Leicester: Inter-Varsity Press

Westermann, Claus (1974/1984) *Genesis 1-11. A Commentary*. E.T. by J.J. Scullion, London: SPCK

Whale, J.S. (1960) *Victor and Victim. The Christian Doctrine of Redemption*. Cambridge U.P.

White, Roger (1982) 'Notes on Analogical Predication and Speaking about God', *The Philosophical Frontiers of Christian Theology. Essays Presented to D.M. MacKinnon*. Edited by B. Hebblethwaite and S.R. Sutherland, Cambridge University Press, pp.197-226

Wittgenstein, Ludwig (1921/1961) *Tractatus Logico-Philosophicus*, E.T. by D.F. Pears and B.F McGuinness, London: Routledge and Kegan Paul

Wittgenstein, Ludwig (1945-9/1958) *Philosophical Investigations*, E.T. by G.E.M. Anscombe, Oxford: Blackwell

World Council of Churches (1982) *Baptism, Eucharist, Ministry. Faith and Order Paper No.111*. Geneva

Yerkes, James (1983) *The Christology of Hegel*. Albany: State University of New York

Yoder, John Howard (1984) *The Priestly Kingdom. Social Ethics as Gospel*. University of Notre Dame Press

Young, Frances (1975) *Sacrifice and the Death of Christ*. London: SCM Press

Zizioulas, John D. (1985) *Being As Communion. Studies in Personhood and the Church*. London: Darton, Longman and Todd

INDEX OF BIBLICAL REFERENCES

INDEX OF SUBJECTS

INDEX OF SUBJECTS

INDEX OF NAMES